Take Flight

The Magic of Reframing Your Experiences to Live an Empowered Life

Lisa Eleni

FOREWORD BY MELISSA KIM CORTER

TAKE FLIGHT
The Magic of Reframing Your Experiences to
Live an Empowered Life

Copyright © 2023. Lisa Eleni

ISBN: 979-8-9885147-7-0

Book Design by
Transcendent Publishing
www.TranscendentPublishing.com

Illustrations by Stevie Famulari, Gds
Author's Photographs by Masha Poland

Printed in the United States of America.

Dedication

To my daughter Kelsie and son Ryan, who have been relentless cheerleaders and constant support and inspiration on my journey to write this book. You have taught me trust, the beauty and power of unconditional love, and the importance of fulfilling dreams with your insights and compassion. You always seem to appear when I need support or time to reconnect to my mission. You help me stretch myself to embrace change and grow, and I trust you implicitly with my heart. You are the reason I was inspired to write this book and I am so grateful we are such an integral part of each other's lives.

Contents

Foreword

*I*n our ever-changing, fast-paced world, it is easy to lose sight of the magic and wonder surrounding us. We get caught up in the demands of daily life, the pressures of work, and the constant stream of information bombarding our senses. In the midst of this chaos, we long for a sense of peace, healing, and connection—to find a way to take flight and soar above the challenges that weigh us down.

It is with great honor that I introduce you to *Take Flight: The Magic of Reframing Your Experiences to Live an Empowered Life*, a magnificent book written by my talented colleague and friend, Lisa Eleni. As I read through the pages of this transformative book, I was immediately reminded of Lisa's powerful presence. Lisa has a unique ability to creatively convey profound wisdom with grace and in a manner that inspires others to find the magic within themselves. Her journey of self-discovery and personal growth is weaved through her words as she invites us to join her on this enchanting path of discovery and healing.

Lisa's creative spirit shines brightly throughout the pages of this book. Each chapter is a testament to her artistic expression and her unique and creative understanding of the human experience. Her writing flows like poetry, painting vivid imagery in our minds and stirring emotions within our hearts. I have had the great privilege and honor of witnessing Lisa transform and grow through various challenges and laughing and sharing the joy of her celebrations. Whether she is exploring the depths of difficult life circumstances or magical experiences of joy and wonder, Lisa's words resonate with authenticity and vulnerability.

What sets Lisa and her book apart from other personal development or spiritual books is her unique approach to healing through creative practices and real-life experiences. Lisa walks her talk and is dedicated to personal growth and the continuous exploration of self, she is a beacon of light, and this book reveals her essence beautifully. Drawing from her own experiences, Lisa has transformed obstacles into potential. As I turned each page, I could clearly feel the power of Lisa's voice; one of her gifts is sharing her story to inspire others to discover their authentic expression.

Throughout the book, Lisa encourages us to embrace our authenticity and to trust the obstacles, limitations, and barriers that appear on the path; she teaches us how to see them differently. Therefore, they take on a purposeful meaning. She reminds us that we are not broken or flawed but rather unique beings capable of immense growth and transformation. With compassion and empathy, she guides us through the metaphorical reflection of a kite, gently coaxing us out of our comfort zones and into the realm of self-discovery.

Take Flight: The Magic of Reframing Your Experiences to Live an Empowered Life is more than just a spiritual guide— it is a call to action. Lisa invites us to step out of our limited perceptions and into a broader understanding of ourselves and the world around us. She challenges us to question our beliefs, to let go of what no longer serves us, and to embrace a mindset of possibility and abundance. Through her words, she ignites a spark within us, reminding us that we are capable of spreading our wings and soaring to new heights.

It is my sincere belief that Lisa's book will touch the hearts and minds of countless readers, offering solace, inspiration, and a path toward personal growth. Whether you are seeking healing, spiritual nourishment, or simply a deeper understanding of yourself and the world, this book is a valuable companion on your journey.

As I reached the final pages of Lisa's book, I found myself sitting in the magic of wonder and creativity; a profound sense of hope washed over me. Lisa's book is a testament to the resilience of the human spirit and the transformative power of the soul. She reminds us that it is safe to trust our inner wisdom and allow the support of the unseen world within and around us. With her gentle guidance and heartfelt words, Lisa leads us toward the light of the soul in an expansive, loving, and graceful way.

I extend my deepest gratitude to Lisa for sharing her wisdom and insights with us. It has been an incredible honor to watch Lisa discover her magic and share it with the world. Her authenticity, vulnerability, and creativity shine through this book, leaving an indelible mark on the reader's soul. This book is evidence of the divine spark within each of us, it so happens the creative nudge moved through Lisa, and she chose to acknowledge and harness that spark; it is a gift of the divine to us through her beautiful perspective, a true talisman, and magical guide for the times we are in.

May *Take Flight: The Magic of Reframing Your Experiences to Live an Empowered Life* be a guiding light for all who venture into its transformative embrace,

–Melissa Kim Corter, International best-selling Author, Teacher & Speaker

Introduction

Welcome, my friend. My hope is that reading about my journey will assist in your own enlightenment and open you up to new possibilities for designing your life. I have had many experiences and excuses for dimming my light, whether it was to avoid conflict or simply just to fit in. I became a master at shutting down and I developed so many coping mechanisms that I wasn't even an active participant in my own life. I was so busy trying to be what I perceived everyone expected me to be that I sabotaged my uniqueness.

For years I carried extra weight, literally and figuratively. While on this journey I had to honestly reflect about what the weight was actually protecting. What I realized is that I had developed unhealthy patterns of being dishonest with myself about what I was feeling in any given situation, and the weight was a physical manifestation of this practice. Rather than incessantly dieting, I intentionally focused more energy on discovering what I was trying to hide from myself and others about who I am and what I want to accomplish in this life. I turned inward and stopped looking for acceptance from external sources. Listening to myself has changed the way I present myself to the world. I have learned to create other tools of protection for myself so I didn't need the weight anymore; I knew it was safe to release it and step into my own authenticity.

I spent years living in fear of what I couldn't control, which seemed like everything at one point or another. This practice put me so far into the future that I wasn't present for each day I was experiencing. Once I did some deep reflection on the patterns and stories I was creating and began to honor my feelings, I was able to shift my mindset for all situations. In this book, I have included some of the most powerful experiences in my personal transformation, which helped me shift my perspective and attitude about my life.

This book is not just about reading my story, but gleaning something from it that connects to your own. There are universal themes here: finding your voice, self-care, embracing love, dealing with separation and isolation, standing in your personal power, facing fear, creating healthy boundaries, reducing triggers, the power of prayer, releasing what needs to be released, creating a tool box, and trusting Divine timing. My hope is that you can identify a pattern in your life that you want to alter so it serves your highest good rather than draining your energy. I believe we are all energetic beings; therefore, it is imperative that you keep your individual energy moving so you can be the best version of you while navigating the human existence.

I have come to understand that I am on this earth to learn and have life experiences that help me expand and grow. Not all of them are pleasant or worth repeating, but I have found that without awareness of these occurrences I continue to repeat the lesson until it is learned. The situation, people, or circumstances may change until the pattern is identified and I am no longer feeling defensive or insecure. I have heard the phrase "being triggered" intermittently in many instances, but did not really understand the significance until I developed an understanding of why the triggers were presenting themselves to me. With the help and guidance of several mentors and teachers, I have created new tools to help me learn from experiences and shift my awareness. I have come to understand what it means to honor the sensations and delve into what I am learning or feeling instead of stuffing emotions. Now I have the awareness of how to move through the experiences and stop the pattern from being recreated which is much more empowering.

Once I realized my emotional responses were actually incentives for me to learn and grow, I was able to identify and reduce triggers from my interactions with people and experiences. As a result, I am more proactive in my life instead of being reactive or trying to anticipate what does not exist. I am more aware of opportunities presenting themselves for me to shine brighter and live a more authentic life. This book shares several of these experiences and how they turned out to be the stepping stones for my growth. To further illustrate these learnings, I use the extended metaphor of a kite.

If you look at a kite, you'll see the basic components that allow it to fly: a spine, crossbar, both sides of the bridle, bridle point, kite line, tail, and the kite itself. As the stories progress, I refer to these parts, connecting each to the corresponding aspect of a person who is balanced in mind, body, and spirit. Once a kite is released and flies freely in the sky; it seems effortless. Similarly, all experiences are much more pleasant when I release control and trust that God, angels, and my mindset is helping me to stay in the flow and trust so that I can reach new heights and fly.

Chapter One

The Joys and Horrors of Kite Flying

Flying kites elicits such a relaxing feeling for me. I think there is a beautiful simplicity to letting out the string to see how high I can get the kite to soar. I used to fly kites with my nana as a child. I have such fun memories of seeing her smiling at me while running around her in a park toting my kite. It was blissful and a great way to find joy in those simple moments with her. As an adult, I wanted to recreate that when I had my own kids. I decided one way to do that was to buy my children kites for every Easter. Living in the upper Midwest, it was always a toss-up as to what kind of weather we would have on Easter – from blustery winds and low temperatures to budding grass and clear skies – however, it was such a fun tradition to go out to the farm and fly kites that we took the risk each year even though there could be a myriad of weather conditions. On sunny spring days with a gentle breeze, the kids would buzz with excitement as they assembled their kites and ran out the door to see them in flight. Listening to them giggle with joy as they ran around the yard, occasionally looking back at their kites trailing behind them, reminded me of those magical days with Nana. The extended family would gather around and cheer them on while I frantically tried to capture these fleeting moments with my video camera.

At some point after the kite took flight, my kids had the calm and peaceful realization that they could just hold the string and enjoy watching the kite shift with the breeze or a gentle tug on the rope. Reeling it in and letting it out as they tried to get their kites close together to share the nice current of wind without getting tangled added an extra challenge. It was almost mesmerizing to see the kite dancing on its own with the breeze. The awareness that the kite was finding its way as it gently roamed the cloudless sky made the day seem brighter and witnessing their unbridled joy at the simplicity of kite flying felt magical.

On years when it was still snowy and cold, the breeze seemed more like a torrential blast swirling uncontrollably, making the flight of the kite extremely difficult, if not impossible. Determined to go for it anyway, the few of us participating would don mittens and warm jackets and head out into the elements to see what would happen. There was optimism in the air and concerted efforts were made to will the kite into submission; however, on those cold stormy years there were always more obstacles to success. They would enjoy the flight for a while, then, without warning, a gust of wind would arise and the kite would dive down into the turf. Trees seemed to be pulling at the strings and entangling the kites into a tight grip among their branches – usually too high to retrieve. Forcing the kites to hang there, lifeless, well into the summer months.

Although there was still laughter, there was also an air of frustration that the kite and various elements would not cooperate. The more control we attempted to exert over the minute details, the more our efforts were met with resistance and perceived problems. Fewer members of the family came those years when the weather was more aligned with winter than spring.

Many members of the family watched from the warmth and safety of the house as we frantically tried to get the kites airborne. Whether they were inside or outside, the family who gathered to watch suddenly became experts on what needed to be done to rectify the countless issues. These included not enough string, meaning the kite did not have the freedom to find the gentle current above to sway so it was forced into the ground without enough time to react. Yanking on the string did not make the kite rise; it would inevitably go directly into the ground, nose first with the determination of a dive bomber, and break. Attempts to straighten the broken bough or tape the ripped plastic and force the kite to perform led to another problem and another potential solution; the kids just needed to run faster.

Not running fast enough made the kite skid along the turf unceremoniously, which led them to pull the string too hard, breaking it. A few more knots in the string seemed an ample fix, which led to a new strategy of trying to jerk the kite so it would go up into the air when the wind was merciless and too gusty. Too much wind made the kite swirl in an awkward lemniscate (infinity) pattern, only to be forced to the ground by another gust. A challenge of wills ensued in the form of taping and repairing, until inevitably the kite was broken to the point that it no longer worked. This was often the point when we gave up and tried another activity to distract us from the defeat.

In truth, I probably wasn't as reflective in my ponderance of what else we could have tried. The excuses piled up about why all of our attempts to control the outcome were futile and relentlessly rejected by the elements, eventually shutting us down. Maybe I should have invested more money in the kite – the cheap plastic ones were no match for the temperamental Midwest climate. Or maybe I should have learned that the repeated failures conditioned me not to even want to bother anymore as I hastily threw the remnants of plastic and string into the trash.

This was a sharp contrast of those sunny years, when I couldn't get enough of the laughter and perceived ease with which the kite was able to fly without incident. Family that gathered enjoyed the simplicity of the temporary joy the kids were eliciting, and no one was inside watching from the windows. They were there on the sidelines enjoying the wonderful spring weather. No one felt the need to shout out suggestions either; they just let the day progress. Even if the string fell onto the ground, the kite still managed to stay in flight; waiting for the child to gather up the remaining ball of string to let it out more. The warm spring air and sun seemed to make the activity much more pleasant for everyone.

No matter what the experience was like for the kids, they never seemed to hold onto the frustration or the joy for very long. They would quickly move on to another activity with their cousins and try something else to entertain themselves with perceivable ease. The adults, however, seemed to wallow in the defeat or rejoice in the merriment, discussing for a good half hour what we should have done differently or reveling in the ease of it all. It occurred to me that the joy of childhood and the nostalgia of childhood are very closely linked for adults. When the kids are smiling and having fun, we are reminded of the simplicity of our youth. When the elements are uncooperative and frustration looms with every choice we make to force the kite to cooperate, the more we hold onto the guilt of not making it happen. Somehow the old stories of disappointment linger in our minds, making us feel like failures. This reflection led me to the a-ha moment that inspired this book.

The kids were getting older and had other interests, and I suspected that this may be our last year of kite flying. Of course, as Easter approached, so did a snowstorm. I spent a little more time and effort picking out some sturdy kites in anticipation of the inclement weather. Sure enough, it turned out to be a cloudy, windy, and cold day, and some of the adults suggested we just skip it. My children, Kelsie and Ryan, disagreed, and I was pretty pumped that I had picked out more resilient kites which seemed to foreshadow inevitable success.

The assembly of the kite was more intricate than previous years, with additional time and thought needed to interpret the cryptic instructions. This kite was not just plastic, but had actual wooden dowels, various glues, and sturdy fabric. As we headed out the door bundled in our mittens and hats, we considered past defeats and how to prevent some of the situations that led to them. One of our most powerful decisions this year was to go out into the field rather than staying by the house; this way, the trees and other interferences could not hamper our success. This relocation made it more difficult for others to watch from the kitchen window, but we knew we had to change up the routine. Wind gusts were temperamental and annoying, but our spirits were high. The kids were older and had some of their own strategies to try without adult intervention. The anticipation of success, despite the brutal weather, became our motivation.

I rolled my eyes when I saw the snowflakes fluttering from the dark clouds. Again, I sensed this was the last year the kids would participate in the kite-flying tradition and felt some attachment to the outcome. I wanted to absorb as much of that child-like enthusiasm as I could before their impending shift into adulthood.

The kids were discussing various strategies to get their kites into the air while I positioned myself along the side of the field. They each had their own and did a countdown to try and coordinate their flights. One kite did a complete nosedive and smashed rather unceremoniously into the turf within the first three minutes of being airborne. The other kite hovered about two feet above the ground before suffering the same fate. There was stifled laughter and a lingering pall of disappointment in the air as they picked up the broken pieces and recapped the demise of the flights. Adult family members began suggesting how to do it right and what they should do next, but by that time the kids were laughing so hard they disregarded the advice. Then they looked at us and said, "We got it," which we correctly interpreted as, "Stop telling us what to do." They wanted to be in control and not have constant intervention from the bystanders.

After a brief meeting of the minds, the kids decided to fly just one of the kites instead of dividing their efforts. They took parts from each to make one good kite, and with an air of determination they discussed the next steps quietly among themselves. Meanwhile, the wind had picked up and the snow started to suck the heat out of the core of my body; my toes were already numb and my nose was incessantly running. Some of the family members were heading in; they felt they were no longer needed or they only saw potential failure. I, however, was so invested that I declined their suggestion to get out of the cold.

Unfazed by the dwindling audience, Kelsie and Ryan devised and executed a new plan in which each had an important role to play. The faster runner would be the one to hold the string and the other one would hold the kite at the perfect tilt to facilitate flight. They waited for the wind gust that swirled snow into their faces before beginning the countdown; then, when they thought the conditions were just right, they let the kite go.

As the string rapidly unfurled from the tight ball, the kite made it up into the air. Even with the wind blowing it in all directions, it stayed above the violent current and swayed back and forth well above our heads. There were celebratory high fives as they both held the string and watched the kite swirl around for a while. Success, even in a storm! It was magical.

I am not sure if I cried that day, but as I sit here years after my children graduated college and went out on their own, I have tears spilling from my eyes at the memory of our kite flying adventures. My emotional release is due in part to the realization that kite flying is a metaphor for my life. The more details I try to control, the more resistance I feel. Sometimes, I am just dragged along the dirt, scuffling as my support sticks are fractured and then I just give up. Or, I am tugged too hard in a direction that is not for my highest good, and my string breaks or the plastic rips, making it harder to fly. This forces me to either build a new kite with the pieces that are still intact and focus on just one kite rather than dividing my attention – just as Kelsie and Ryan did that stormy day.

In this portion of the metaphor, the kite is a symbol for my goals and dreams. When I put time into building a strong kite, with elements in place that will sustain the flight no matter what comes my way, I am much more content to find the breeze, even if there is choppy weather. If I work toward my goals with consistency and clarity, there isn't as much difficulty when all the elements fall into place. Dreams are wonderful to conjure up, and they need to be coupled with small action steps. It is important to determine what the next step toward my goal will be along the journey. I don't have to have the plan and all of the elements mapped out to begin. I find that if I try to predict everything that can potentially prevent my success, I get mired down by the extraneous details and self-sabotage, which only makes that success harder to achieve. Sometimes I even give up altogether. However, if I just take one small step and leave room for a change or improvement in my plan, things unfold much more easily.

If my intentions don't align with my highest good, I often need some time and maybe a few alterations to my plan. This is a great time to reflect and regroup. Whether I am crying or laughing at my perceived failure, I have to honor what I am feeling and get clarity about what needs to be shifted. Then, from this new perspective, I try again. Sometimes, I just need to reflect on why my kite didn't take flight, or why my goals were not coming together the way that I had hoped – perhaps because of poor construction, cheap parts, or unforeseen events. All have contributed to a new version or attempt at flying; I just need to revamp my approach or learn a lesson before moving to the next attempt.

The takeaway here is that when manifesting, the journey itself not only contributes to the outcome but is often more important. I might want something to come together, but it doesn't always. Each perceived setback is actually the magic hour when I need to either recalibrate or heal so I can reconstruct a better, sturdier version of my goals – and myself. Sometimes I don't succeed with my original plan so something better that I wasn't considering can take shape.

It's also important to be aware of my "bystanders" and what they bring to the plan. I know that some people are back in the house choosing not to participate because it's too cold, or too windy and there is too much effort. In other words, they believe my dreams won't be successful anyway so they don't need to be next to me in inclement weather. There are others who shout out what I should be doing, or not doing, which diverts my attention or makes me second guess what I am doing rather than relying on my own intuition. Those are the naysayers and dream-stealers. Oftentimes their suggestions are based on their own fears, and listening to them or absorbing their negativity can deter me from living my journey with authenticity and excitement. This book would have never come to fruition if I didn't stop listening.

When I just find a way to incorporate the lessons I learned in my previous attempts, make one good, sturdy kite, and let those who support me help coordinate my efforts, I can fly no matter what weather or obstacle is in my way. Even if I have failed before, and people around me have lost interest or left me somewhere along the way, I do not have to stop trying. New people who are more aligned with my success do appear – every time. Sometimes my dreams have to change or be released so a new vision can become clearer. It doesn't mean I am giving up or slumping down into victimhood, I am just changing my goals since the unforeseen events, like stormy weather, made me rethink what I really want. The storms of my life have been some of my greatest teachers. Once I started to realize that the storm was actually clearing out new space for my dreams to flourish, I took the time to refocus and stay motivated to create the life I want. I was able to resist the need to hold onto people or control situations that were actually life-lessons to keep me aligned with my highest good.

As a result, I have become a very sturdy, beautiful kite capable of sharing awareness, amazing gifts, and lessons that I have experienced. I had to learn to trust in myself and know that I am guided and loved unconditionally which took time and a lot of reflection to get enough clarity about what to shift and when. I had to work on some of my shadows and doubts so I would no longer be overrun by them and find the sunny days (even within the storms) to manifest my dreams. I also had to trust Divine timing. Forcing my kite by tugging on the string or fighting the breeze led to failure each time. Sometimes it is important to loosen the grip on what I try to anticipate and let life unfold, trusting that I am guided and I am right where I am supposed to be, even if it is uncomfortable. I still work toward my goals, I just don't panic when it isn't going exactly to my plan.

Let's go back to the kite metaphor. Choosing myself is the spine of the kite, as this is the most important piece of the whole structure. Since l will spend my whole life with me, I need to learn how to listen, reflect, grow, and nurture myself along the way so I become balanced in mind, body, and spirit. A thirst for knowledge and discernment about what mentors I rely upon are the cornerstones of my development and ever-growing toolbox of strategies. Listening to my body and caring for myself also requires diligence and compassion for myself so I can clear my mind and balance my spirit.

What I have learned is that when I do not practice selfcare, I become a spectator in my own life because I am out of alignment. The term "selfcare" is not only the occasional massage or weekend getaway, but encompasses a spiritual practice of reflection and honoring your feelings, desires, and dreams. Letting others control you or resisting the joy and experiences that you are here on the earth to learn and grow from are self-sabotaging and will literally suck the life out of you. The drain on your personal energy will inhibit your ability to use that energy to move forward in other areas of your life that need it.

It is also imperative that you not only give your time and energy to those you love but open up and receive the love others are trying to give you. This is an essential awareness that gives me so much abundance and joy. So many times, I have unintentionally cut people off by insisting I'm okay or that I can "just do it," even if it was more difficult for me to be successful alone. I now believe that people come into my path for a specific purpose, and I am not so quick to dismiss encouragement or guidance.

Loved ones are here to support my growth in a myriad of ways. Some interactions are not pleasant, but they are just as pivotal to my expansion. When I am triggered or uncomfortable, I know it is my sign that I have some healing to do. Consequently, people fall away or stay to remind me that it is time to shift some aspect of my awareness. These learning opportunities help me create new boundaries to prevent being sabotaged by negativity. I am often more inclined to recalibrate and get myself centered when I reflect on what I am experiencing in these unpleasant situations. Sometimes I have to reach out for help to get a different perspective, and sometimes I can do it for myself by shifting the way I am integrating the experience. Once the lesson is learned, I am able to release the confusion and move forward into a new space. As difficult as that can be for me, I realized that some people come into my life to show contrast, and some come to mirror what I want to create. What's more, new people consistently come along who are more aligned with my current energy. I get to choose who I will collaborate with, just as my children did while kite-flying during the storm. They had the same goal, and once they blocked out suggestions from bystanders, they were able to re-calibrate their plan, so it aligned with that goal. Since I am learning from the experiences, I also need to be mindful of how I integrate what I am learning and recalibrating what my goals are.

To navigate our path with more clarity, we must learn to reflect and decide when we want outside suggestions and when we need to follow our own intuition. Cultivating this discernment was a challenge for me. Like Kelsie and Ryan, I had to figure out what I could do on my own and when I needed to be open to other people shouting out their suggestions from the sidelines. To make the kite functional support has to be created; however, we must first be open to hearing guidance in its various forms. Some support will come from outside assistance such as a trusted friend or mentor; sometimes it comes from the highest source of my faith – God, my spiritual guides, and loved ones. Each situation necessitates some time for me to figure out what I need to learn and whose ideas I will incorporate. It is my choice to listen to advice and to filter through suggestions from others that may deflect me from getting my kite to fly.

The first lesson I had to integrate was to make myself a priority. After all, I am the only one who can control my reactions, make my reflections about what is happening to me, and learn and grow from each experience. Surprisingly, this was a very difficult shift for me to make. I needed the awareness of how I was self-sabotaging and denying myself the freedom to live my life with joy, not just my responsibilities.

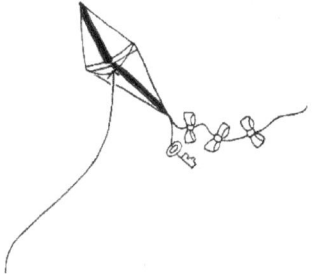

Chapter Two

It is Not Selfish to Choose Yourself
(The Spine of Your Kite)

The time when your kids transition out of your home and leave you with an empty nest, is truly life-changing. After years of tending to my son and daughter's every need, I was suddenly barely seeing them, which was a very jarring transition. I was ecstatic when, after months away at college, they announced they were coming home to visit me and attend a family event. The joy I felt, however, existed alongside a deep sadness related to that event.

My nephew, with whom I had been very close throughout his life, was getting married. I have so many memories of watching him growing up, from cheering him on at his T-ball and basketball games to seeing him coach my son's little league team for two seasons. Seeing him become such a wonderful young man filled me with pride. He finished his college degree and fell in love, and I was so excited to see that he had found his footing and was moving into an amazing life that I knew he dreamed of. The wedding was going to be such a beautiful celebration…the problem was, I was not invited to attend the festivities.

This was the first family event since my divorce, and the message was sent: I had left the whole family, not just my ex-husband. Being excluded from the wedding after being so present in my nephew's life triggered a lot of heartache, but it also ignited several inciteful realizations. This weekend is when I learned the most important element to move forward with my life after divorce and living on my own for the first time since I left my home for my own college experiences. I had to create my future and put my needs and desires first instead of trying to recreate the past. This was a new path for me, and an overwhelming one, because there were now voids in my life I did not know how to fill. The deep sadness I felt welling up in my throat was juxtaposed with the absolute joy I felt knowing the kids would be coming home to spend some time with me between the wedding events. Having my kids around that weekend made it easier to step into the old role of mothering I knew so well, but somehow it was no longer a good fit.

The kids arrived and my daughter wanted a manicure, so we set off to the mall. We passed the pet store and headed into the nail salon, chatting about her latest college adventures and catching up. It felt so good to be around her and share in her excitement. I tried to stay in the moment and soak it up without dwelling on the fact that this was a quick trip. I was counting on the time together to be cathartic and rejuvenating for us.

As we exited the nail salon, I could feel my heart skip as I looked across the hall. For some inexplicable reason, I was compelled to stop at the pet store on the way out of the mall. I couldn't understand why there was such a pull for me. I had never felt this urge any of the countless times before when I made my way to the parking lot. I just had to visit the cute animals in the pet store. I had adopted two kittens from a local shelter to keep me company after my divorce, so I certainly did not need any pets. My conscious mind kept asking, *What are you doing?* but my heart kept telling me to go in and look. Before I knew it, I was in front of the window watching the adorable puppies romping around in their spaces. My daughter had one quick errand to take care of before we left the mall, which gave me some time to kill. I moved in from the doorway, and that is when I saw them; two Shiba Inu puppies – one blonde and one red like a baby fox – relaxing on the top of their food dish, despite all the toys randomly strewn about the cage.

I couldn't believe how adorably the brother and sister had curled up together. Just watching their little chests slowly rising and falling made my heart beat a little faster. When their patient, deep brown eyes met mine, something shifted. I felt like I was connected to them and I had no desire to look at any of the other animals.

A kind lady standing next to me interrupted my reverie. She told me that they were her puppies and proceeded to tell me the story of how they ended up here at the pet store. She assured me she wasn't a breeder and that when her dog became pregnant, she realized she couldn't keep all seven in the litter.

Her heart was heavy letting them go but she thought she could find them good homes by bringing them to the pet store. The way they had looked right through me to the depths of my heart seemed like a sign; meeting this woman, I felt, was another. I just wanted to nurture them and keep them safe. I felt a pressing need to cuddle them so I asked if I could take them to the other room.

The assistant brought me to a small room, which smelled like a horrid mix of new puppies, cat urine and sanitizer. For the next fifteen minutes I fidgeted in a chair with a lump in my throat and tears stinging my eyes as I waited for her to bring them in. I knew this was not a rational thing to be doing, but I just couldn't seem to stop myself.

The door creaked open and the puppies ran for my chair, wagging their entire bodies with pure excitement. Watching them ignited the anticipation in me as well. The attendant told me that the blonde puppy was the female and the red one was her brother. She then helped them onto my lap, instantly sealing my attachment. It was reminiscent of holding my children for the first time and I felt a warmth travel through my body. My emotions were high, and I was completely immersed in the moment.

I could feel the excitement in their bodies as they squirmed relentlessly up my chest and reached to my face to give me kisses. They were in constant motion, pawing over each other to kiss my neck and wiggle their tails. They were so full of life and optimism which contrasted the sadness I was feeling in this new stage of my life. How could I leave without them? My rational self asked how I would manage, but my emotional self had a ready response to all of my queries. I had a great back yard. I could fence them in and let them run around. We had created a bond of love in moments and knew in my heart that I couldn't risk them being separated or sent to other homes. When my daughter returned, I told her that I couldn't leave them, she smiled and held onto them as I filled out the paperwork.

With the adoption complete, I set off to my house to get everyone settled. The puppies were so sweet and cuddly and kept giving me kisses on the way home. My children created a special place for them to be in the entryway with several cushions and toys and a nice place to acclimate themselves to their new space. It was adorable to see them cuddle and sleep curled next to each other. Both of my kids were excited, and we all agreed that they were ridiculously adorable and sweet. The fact that they were siblings was an added bonus.

My cats were used to my daughter's dog being around, so I didn't think the transition would be too traumatic for them. I bought new leashes and named the male Nikko and his sister Nala. My cats weren't too bothered by our new friends initially. None of them seemed too interested or annoyed with each other so I figured we would all get along just fine. Just watching the brother and sister playing together brought me an almost overwhelming wave of joy.

The kids went to do some quick last-minute wedding errands, leaving me beaming at the new puppies. I decided to announce the arrival of my new companions to my girlfriends and did so with a flurry of phone calls. They didn't react the way I thought they would, and I started to get a pang of remorse about my spontaneous decision. So many red flags started to pop up, but I didn't quite see the whole picture and I ignored my feelings of doubt. Watching the puppies play with reckless abandon and excitement seemed to surpass my fears. With every red flag, I had a justification of how this situation would be awesome, but I was just fooling myself. I was so caught up in the moment that I was able to see plausible solutions that I thought would be ample.

My best friend was shocked. The only thing that divided her and her boyfriend was having to care for their dog. She often complained that she always had to take care of her and how much work it was. She had a hard time scheduling her free time because the dog was like an infant and needed constant care. Maybe her dog was just lonely, I thought. When I was teaching at school my puppies would be able to entertain each other and wouldn't be lonely – especially since I had such a nice yard for them to run around in.

After that phone call, I took the puppies outside to play with their new toys. Moments later, I had to go to my neighbor's door to retrieve a ball, which had unceremoniously flown over the fence dividing our yards. I brought the puppies with me and introduced them to the neighbor's kids, aged three and six.

"They are brother and sister, just like you," I told them.

"Good luck," their mother said, "They will probably fight constantly!"

I reflected back to my own children and figured Nikko and Nala would get along as well as they did. After all, they seemed to have mild dispositions. Thinking there was no reason to take on that negativity, I simply thanked the neighbor for getting the toy from their yard. Time would reveal that this was just another red flag that I justified ignoring.

The hour of my nephew's wedding was fast approaching, and my kids were almost ready to go. My heart felt a bit of a sting at the reality of not being included and I was happy the dogs were going to be there to keep my mind off the event. I put on a brave face as my son asked me to iron the wrinkled shirt he pulled from the pit of his suitcase. While I worked, we talked about his friends and various new interests he was exploring in college, and by the time I got the final creases in his collar I could feel the nostalgia pulsing through me.

After taking a few photos of them all dressed up, I dropped them off at the wedding venue and my house was quiet once again. I went into the backyard to join the puppies. I noticed the little gold one, Nala, was starting to dig in the soft dirt rather aggressively in the budding garden. Ugh, that was going to be a problem, I thought. My friend called moments later asking to bring her daughter over so she could get her "puppy fix." Absolutely, I said, any time. She proceeded to tell me that her husband always had Sheba Inus growing up and that they are known for being escape artists. This meant they would dig in my yard and could potentially dig by the fence to escape. The puppies could end up in my neighbor's yard or worse, in the busy street. Anxiety started to build. What if they constantly got out and I couldn't keep them safe? I could envision my not-too-distant future of repeatedly going to the pound to pick them up. I began to wonder why I had put this burden on myself.

This was the first of a flurry of heart-wrenching questions that hadn't occurred to me when I was sitting in the pet store. My kids were going back to college – who would I call when I needed help keeping the puppies content? What would happen when the school year started and I went back to work? What if I want to go to a game after school to watch my students? I would have to rush home and take care of the dogs and would most likely just stay home for the evening.

I remembered doing that for my pets when I was married. Having a twenty-minute commute made it difficult to meet up with friends after work or watch my students' school events because I had to hurry home to let the dogs out. On a few occasions, I would call a neighbor to let them out so I wouldn't miss my own kids' events. Now, post-divorce and living in this new neighborhood, I had no one to ask for help. My mind started reeling and that's when my joy over these sweet, brown-eyed babies turned into anxiety and regret.

As the evening wore on and the puppies got more comfortable with their new surroundings, a shift in their personalities alarmed me. They started to bark at each other and did not play as well. One started nipping at my cat and the other was chasing my other cat around the house. The tension amongst four of them was palpable, and my joy and enthusiasm was giving way to dread of the oppressive responsibility I had taken on. The puppies were biting at the carpet and scratching at their gate as the evening settled in, so I let them out into the backyard where they continued to dig and nip at each other. I tried to engage them with one of their toys, but they were oblivious to my presence. As I made my way back into the house, both of my cats had their ears back and I felt a lump in my throat. This affected them too. I knew I had some tough decisions to make, and that night I lay awake for hours trying to work out all of the extraneous details my emotional self hadn't considered before bringing Nikko and Nala home.

The kids were having great experiences in their respective colleges and their lives were moving on for them. Mine had seemed to stall – newly divorced, and not really needed by my children on a daily basis. I missed the busyness of my life. I missed going to the games and hanging out with the other parents as we cheered on our budding athletes and musicians. I missed cooking for my kids and hanging out with them as they gave me updates on what was transpiring throughout their days and the other kids that I knew. Now my heart was heavy, and I was feeling lost and sad.

As the hours passed and I envisioned what the next twelve to fifteen years might look like, my anxiety started to churn in my gut. I was perplexed about what to do next, and was frantically scrambling for some semblance of a plan. Kelsie and Ryan came home and, after sharing many colorful details of the wedding and reception, they asked how it was going with the new puppies. I tried to remain casual as I told them of the shift in the temperament of the puppies, how I didn't think that I could take care of them, and wasn't sure what to do about the situation I had created. I started to cry as I recounted my evening, though I suspected the tears were not only about the puppies, and I think my kids knew that too. I apologized to them, saying that I was considering taking Nikko and Nala back to the pet store so they could have a better home with a young family. Kelsie and Ryan assured me that they understood and wouldn't want me to be burdened when they couldn't be around to help. Hearing this, I started to feel a little bit less anxious, but I still had to wrestle with the guilt I was feeling and be more practical about my options.

I needed to get my emotions out of my processing and really consider what I wanted. I had to come to the realization that I had made a very emotional decision that had long-lasting effects on how my life was going to shape up with all of my new changes. When I had puppies before, my kids were little, and having them grow up with pets taught them so much about responsibility and unconditional love that it didn't seem as burdensome to have them. Now I was looking at a very fuzzy version of my life and diverting my attention to reflect on all of the responsibility of having two new puppies was not in my best interest. As I talked it over with my kids, we agreed that these pets deserved to be happier in a home with younger children and more people who could help care for them. I realized that the pet store's 24-hour policy was in place for a reason, and I needed to act fast and consider what was best for everyone.

Once my decision was made, time seemed to creep along at a sloth's pace. As it approached the hour that the pet store opened, I continually had to remind myself that having these rambunctious puppies wasn't the best plan for everyone in-volved. I wanted them to have a good life… with someone else. I couldn't disrupt my life while I was still recalibrating from life-altering changes; nor could I do that to my cats. With a guilt-ridden heart, I called the store as soon as the clock struck nine a.m. and they let me bring them back. I apologized pro-fusely to the puppies on the car ride to the mall. They were squirming in my lap and biting my face and fingers. My heart was filled with sadness, but I knew it was the right thing to do for all of us. I just kept hoping that they would have a good life and prayed they would forgive me for taking them back to the store. Then it occurred to me that it wasn't a coincidence that I had adopted them on the weekend of my nephew's wedding.

I was feeling abandoned and lost without my kids in my empty nest. I had defined myself as a mother and a wife for twenty years, but now that those roles had shifted my life seemed to lack meaning and clarity. I knew Kelsie and Ryan were enjoying their new adventures, and part of me was thrilled for them. In contrast, the other part of me was desperately lonely and sad that I wasn't an integral part of their lives any-more. I felt disconnected from the life that I had created with them and I was having a hard time finding my footing now that two main components of what I drew my happiness and much of my identity from were no longer options.

I was always busy in my head and in my daily routine keeping track of all of our schedules. I had been so conditioned to make them a priority in my life that I rarely put myself first.

The phone calls from them were great, but they didn't

have the same feeling of connection. I always knew their childhood friends but now the new people in their lives were faceless. It was a lot to adjust to in addition to a divorce which had resulted in a shift in my social circle as well. I was overwhelmed trying to figure how I would redefine myself and grasping to feel some enthusiasm for my life. Reflecting on this, I started to understand my pull to adopt the puppies. I felt the need to protect and nurture the little brother and sister just as I had my own children. I wanted to maintain the role of nurturer because it was comfortable and I found it rewarding and exciting. I didn't want the sibling puppies to be separated either. Now I realize it was important to me that my children had each other in college. They weren't separated, but had dinner together quite often and hung out in the same places, while I sat in my empty house.

These puppies came into my life, for a very short time, to teach me the most important lesson about moving forward. I needed to shift my thinking and this weekend was the epiphany that sparked my journey into choosing myself. I had to retrain myself on the nuances of freedom.

I reflected to myself that their graduation was a celebration of their accomplishments and 18 years of the most intensive job I have ever had, but now it is ok to let it go and put myself first. It is not selfish or arrogant; it is just creating a new normal. I had to allow it to come to fruition. I will still be their mother and always do my best to listen to and guide them when they need it, but their level of need will never be the same as it once was. I needed to let them go to new places and have experiences so they could continue growing independently. I also had to reconcile the idea that my role is more of a tertiary one now that they are older. I had to let them become their own adult version of themselves which wasn't as hands-on anymore. I had to stop thinking for my children and let them have their own experiences so they could be functioning adults. By default, I also had to recognize that I also could start doing that for myself.

This is when I chose to care and nurture myself for the first time as an adult in my life. I let myself be creative about what my new chapter could look like if I gave myself permission. I suddenly realized it was okay that other people were watching over my children and spending time with them. That was no longer my daily job. I would be available when they needed me, but I didn't have to take care of their every need. Instead of seeing this as a loss, I could enjoy the fact that I had free time with no restraints or extraneous responsibilities. There was no need to be sad about being alone any longer. If I embraced the changes, I could really be more empowered to live my life in a new way. I could come and go and be with friends or at student activities whenever I wanted.

Change, while unavoidable, is not inherently bad; I simply had to choose how to feel about it. I needed to shift my thinking out of victim mode and choose to find joy in new beginnings. It was time to embrace this new opportunity and not revert back to the familiar more comfortable path that I had traveled raising these children. We had all grown and changed and it was time for me to redefine my priorities. That wasn't an easy shift to make in my current mental state, but once I released the old roles that no longer fit me, I was more able to be open to what could lie ahead.

With the newfound clarity I gained that weekend, I set an intention to get out of the depression and anxiety of wondering what was next for me and begin to nurture myself and find new interests to manifest more joy in my life. The kids became my role models for trying new things and getting excited about the new people and adventures that they were experiencing. I began to go to retreats and outings and meeting new friends. I began filling up my life and myself in a variety of new ways which afforded me new opportunities to really step into a new version of me as an adult. It was one of the most monumental shifts that I made consciously in my life as I began to follow a new path of independence. My head was no longer stuffed with the itineraries of three people. I could just take care of myself. It was liberating.

This is the vertical support, or spine, of my kite. I am the most integral part of my own life, and it is my choice to be victimized or to be empowered. I had to shift my energy from being drained by what was no longer my daily routine to being invigorated by the new adventures I actually had time to embark on. I didn't have to keep running from work to activities and aligning all the hectic family schedules to have self-worth. I could nurture my new relationships and interests without being strangled by trying to maintain who I was in the past. It was quite an epiphany. Struggling to resist the move forward was like yanking on the kite string in a storm; it was futile. When I chose myself, I was able to free myself from the trees that snarled my kite.

This was the start of an amazing new adventure in which I stepped into a new version of myself. I gave myself permission to try new experiences and take on new roles to replace the previous roles that I had become comfortable with. I stretched myself to understand what I like and feel and fed the desire to explore new options to create in this new chapter of my life. This version was not easy for people who knew me to accept, but it was more authentic; it is who I am at my core. I released the confines of what others thought of me or expected from me and freed myself to be myself with the new people who were excited to be with me.

This shift has made the transition to the new me and new normal an amazing adventure. It was not ok for me to stop living my life. In fact, it was the first time my life was actually being fully orchestrated by me. I had to decide to enjoy it as I participated in different activities and reconnected with my soul purpose. This weekend was the rebirth of my life and I owe it all to the little puppies that stole my heart in the pet store.

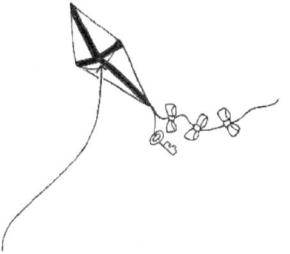

Chapter Three

Give Your Love Selflessly and Allow Others to Do the Same for You
(The Horizontal Bar of Your Kite)

*G*randma Alice was my children's great-grandmother. When she moved into an apartment in our small town, the children and I made it a ritual to visit her every Thursday. When the weather was nice, we walked, stopping along the way to pick a bouquet of wild daisies that Grandma Alice would put in a small vase. On the cold, snowy days, we would take the car and do some errands for her. The kids would sit on her lap and eat her freshly baked muffins and then sing along with a Barney video while Grandma kicked my butt playing her favorite card game, "Spite and Malice." She would laugh at their light-up shoes that blinked while the kids were dancing around the living room, but her focus always remained on the cards. It was a marvel how she could stay so attentive to the game and at the same time completely enjoy the playfulness of the children. I loved every minute of it.

Our conversations were full of humorous recollections of her growing up on the family farm. Her memories ranged in years as much as they did in emotion, and her eyes would gaze into the distance as she recalled some of the more poignant moments. We also teared up at the memories of loss or pain that had a little sting to them. I found commonalities in our experiences: the teenage angst of being too old to be young and too young to be old, along with the many firsts – injuries, loves and losses. All topics seemed timeless. She was an amazing link to the family history, and her accounts of the popular shenanigans of the 1940s and 1950s still makes me laugh today.

When she ended up with pneumonia in February, I had a sinking feeling. She was in her mid-90s and my heart felt heavy when hearing the news. Her chances of recovery were slim, and that harsh reality was draining the color from our family members' faces who had all gathered after being notified of her illness. Each family took turns at her bedside; the rest of us sat in awkward silence in the hall, waiting for our turn and not really knowing how to comfort ourselves or anyone else from the impending grief. My children were a welcome distraction, but even they could feel that something wasn't right and sat quietly beside me.

I brought the kids into her room with me so they could say goodbye. I knew they were much too young to understand the enormity of the situation, other than, Great-grandma is sick. I told them to hug her and tell her they loved her. I clasped her hand and looked into her eyes, stifling my own tears, as I told her how much I loved our card games – even if I really never won. She smiled and gave my hand a light squeeze, grateful for my attempt at levity. Our time with her was nearly over, and the dam I had on my emotions was just about to break. There just didn't seem to be enough air in the room to force down the lump surging up from my heart. I knew that this was going to be a life-changing event, for all of us. What I didn't realize is that she also had an amazing life-changing gift for me.

Grandma Alice often sat next to me in our family pew at church and repeatedly said she loved listening to me sing. My training was limited to being in the high school choir and I alternately chuckled at and dismissed her praise. Whenever I sang, I would see her smiling over at me and I always smiled back reluctantly. Most of the parishioners in our church sang very quietly or just mouthed the words, so I figured she was just pointing out that she could hear me. Once I knew the songs I figured if I sang then the other people around me would be braver and sing a little louder, which seemed to work. In any event, I thought Grandma was just being sweet.

In the dark silence of a cold winter dawn, I was sitting lost in meditation when the phone rang. Only one reason someone was calling at eight a.m., and that's to let me know Grandma Alice had passed. My mother-in-law gave me the details and said Grandma had asked that I sing her favorite hymn, "On Eagles Wings" at her funeral. "Of course," was my immediate response. I couldn't really say no to her final request and I didn't want to. I loved her dearly, and my desire to be a part of her celebration of life and honor her sweet request was a heartfelt one. I couldn't imagine not going to her house with the kids anymore. However, as the rehearsals got under way in the empty church in the days leading up to the funeral, fear began to replace my altruism.

My throat grew increasingly tight and I struggled during rehearsals to hit the high notes. I was getting very tense about singing alone in front of the whole congregation. I had never been a soloist at such an emotionally charged event, and I was overwhelmed with emotions over losing Grandma. I was getting so nervous that my throat was feeling more constricted each day as her funeral approached.

The funeral was held on an overcast and bitterly cold February morning, somewhat fitting for the emotional day that lay ahead. I was a complete bundle of nerves, and just looking out over the empty pews made me shake as I practiced one more time before the parishioners arrived. I knew the service was about to start, but I lagged behind to share a private moment with Grandma Alice while the church was still empty.

Her ornate coffin was draped with fragrant white roses and surrounded by various plants and flowers from friends and family. I decided to take a few precious moments before her celebration of life to be in the silence together. As the musicians made their final preparations, I read some of the touching and poignant cards. I made my way over to the center of the altar where Grandma Alice was positioned for the service. She looked at peace, which was a bit of a contrast from our last time together. No tubes or wires – just her signature red lipstick against the porcelain skin of her face. Her hair was perfectly coiffed and fresh polish was on her nails. I gently slid my hand under hers, which lacked the tenderness and warmth I associated with her touch. I gave it a little squeeze and told her I would do my best to honor her and prayed to God to help me sing the high notes with some grace. I heard the rustling behind me as the parishioners began to come in and made my way down the back stairs to sit with the other musicians, wiping the tears from my eyes.

The church was quiet as family and musicians gathered in a small room filled with whispered voices and the gentle hum of the boiler. Above us, the congregation of friends and family filed into the pews. To distract ourselves from the welling of emotions, we looked at the black and white class confirmation pictures, now faded from years of sun exposure, on the wall. Generations of my husband's family, including Grandma Alice as a young girl and her late husband, were scattered among the photos. The musty smell of the staircase from years of water damage was overpowered by the hot lunch that the church ladies were preparing to serve following the service.

As the time to head up the back stairs approached, my fear made me nauseous. Panic was settling in my abdomen while the family and I sat in the family room and waited to join the other mourners. When the musicians were told to head out, I left the family behind since we had to be in seated in different areas of the sanctuary. As I followed the other musicians up the back stairs, I could feel that the mood had changed in the room since we had practiced earlier. There was a somber pall that filled the air. As the choir began the opening songs, I knew there was no turning back.

I sang along with the rest of the congregation to warm up my voice, but it did nothing to ease my nerves. Instead, as the service began, I found myself repeatedly scanning the program, which was becoming quite wrinkled in my shaking hands, as I waited for my solo, "On Eagle's Wings."

After the touching sermon recounting a life well lived and a sweet poem read by my niece, there was not a dry eye in the church. Then it was my turn. My legs felt stiff as I walked toward the microphone positioned by the piano. *Breathe...*I kept repeating in my head. I was sweating but my feet were cold, and the high heels were not helping to smooth my gait. The horrific embarrassment of squeaking my clarinet in my sixth-grade concert lurched forward from the recesses of my memory as my accompanist winked at me and started the intro.

Throwing up a few more pleas to God, I tried to relax and let the familiarity of the piano music calm me. When I started singing, I followed every word on the sheet music, even though I knew the song by heart. Suddenly, a waft of white roses filled my nose, though they were over ten feet away from me – as if Grandma was reminding me of her special request. I shifted my weight as the inevitable high notes grew closer; then, as I headed into the crescendo, I felt a slight chill down the back of my neck, even though the rest of my body was surging with nervous energy. I closed my eyes to ignore the crowd and the sheet music and could see Grandma's face smiling at me like she had done in church so many times. That's when I finally felt my body start to relax. I was no longer aware of anyone in the room, and I felt the remaining tension drain out of me as I nailed the high notes at the end of Grandma Alice's favorite hymn.

I was aware of the silence in the room when the piano struck the last note of the song. I opened my eyes and paused to let them readjust and acclimate myself. It was then that the lights in the old country church flickered. My accompanist winked at me and a wave of relief came over me as I took the first deep breath since I'd agreed to sing the solo.

As I turned away from the microphone and looked over at the white casket draped in roses, I felt peaceful. How I managed to keep my emotions in control while listening to the sniffles that echoed in the sanctuary is still a mystery to me. The congregation was lost in their own reflections as the musicians and I sang a variety of hymns together to close the ceremony.

When it was over, the mourners systematically filed downstairs for the meal, while I followed the other musicians down the back stairs. The first glimpse of the family was my father-in-law, who was seated at one of the tables with the rest of the immediate family. He was a military man and often rather stoic, especially in emotionally charged situations. He was also known for being concise with his words. He walked directly to me and put his hands on my shoulders. "Beautiful" was all he said, but I could see the sincerity in his eyes. As I returned his embrace, all the tension that had accumulated in the core of my body dissipated. In that moment, my perspective shifted. Although I wanted to honor her wishes and sing for her, I realized then that I received a valuable gift from Grandma Alice in return.

I wasn't very confident about my singing; or much of anything I did, up to that point in my life. I would almost try to talk people out of any compliment because I didn't like the attention to be on me. If someone thought I had a cute outfit on, I would point out that I got it on sale and immediately pay them a return compliment to deflect any kindness. But something changed in me after I honored Grandma Alice's request. I had several people comment on my singing that day. I wasn't really prepared to be complimented; I just wanted to do a good job to honor her and not embarrass myself or the family. I was scared to death to stand in front of the skinny microphone and sing by myself for so many people, especially on such a sad day. It was definitely a big stretch singing alone rather than getting drowned out in a huge congregation and I got so caught up in my head with self-doubt that I didn't even consider that anyone would enjoy it, but they did.

Success was not a guarantee, especially in the state of mind I had contorted myself into with the stress of singing in front of the family and the rest of the town that attended that day. Just as I got to those high notes, I knew the smell of roses was her presence – and reassurance that she was enjoying it – and I felt a shift. I had to close my eyes and sing from my heart, rather than remain in my head concerned with potential failure and ridicule. I needed to reframe my thinking. Once I let my song be a gift for Grandma Alice, I didn't have trouble hitting those high notes and the flickering lights seemed to be a sign from her that she heard me and all the others honoring her memory in her childhood country church. That experience, and the fact that I survived it, opened so many other doors for me. I was challenged to feel from my heart more rather than thinking from my head.

Following this event, I was asked to be lead singer for congregation in our home church and when it came time for me to sing, I was no longer nervous. I felt more empowered and comfortable in my own skin. I have Grandma Alice to thank for opening my heart to receive as well as give because she saw the light in me before I ever knew there was a spark. I never would have pushed myself past the paralyzing fears about singing for anyone else in the world. It was because of her that I realized I needed to be afraid and do it anyway. All of those uncomfortable feelings that welled up within me became irrelevant when I was done because so much had shifted for me.

This amazing expansion taught me that there really is no reason to spend so much time in fear and self-doubt; it was time to live from my heart, rather than my head, to find more joy. Too often, I shied away from kindness and compassion. It didn't occur to me that something I had within me could be shared to give joy or comfort to others. Even when Grandma Alice smiled at me at church, I didn't let it sink in that she was being sincere, not just kind.

I also needed to let love in and receive instead of always giving. I reflected on how I would feel if no one let me help or support them. It is an even exchange when I consciously allow others to express their love to me, not just dismiss or downplay it. Energy flows both ways.

Being open to others expressing their concern, love, and compassion and really letting it into my core has been a complete game-changer for me. Just because I can do something by myself doesn't mean I always have to. What I realized is that I did not feel worthy of help or praise. Somewhere along the line I had internalized the notion that letting others help or support me was a burden to them. Once I had the awareness of that old story I had floating around in my head for years, I was able to rewrite the monologue that was blocking my ability to receive. I have learned that most people really want to be helpful and when I shut them out it essentially makes it impossible for them to express love in their own unique way. I had unintentionally pushed love away because of my own insecurities around worthiness. I had to shift my thoughts so I could be a receiver as well as a giver. I certainly wouldn't want anyone to do that to me, and this is the awareness that I needed to stop doing it to myself.

I also had to honor my feelings of nervousness and finish the task despite those feelings. My new mantra became, "When I am nervous, be of service." I can be uncomfortable and still be successful. When I stop swirling in self-doubt and just let my body relax and trust that I can accomplish the task at hand, I do. Singing became a new way for me to connect with people – a beautiful exchange of energy – and, with this new perspective, I began to let myself embrace the experience.

This is the horizontal support of my kite. The cross structure that stretches the fabric, like open arms receiving a hug, which suggests the importance of being open to receive. This was a big lesson for me. I believe we all have gifts and ways of expressing joy, appreciation, and love. When I downplayed my own worth to others, I was denying them the joy of sharing their love with me. It wasn't intentional; in fact, I never looked at it that way until I had this experience. My instinct to impulsively answer yes to Grandma Alice's request without even a second thought is indicative of my personality. I will drop anything to help those I love, in any way I can. What I didn't consider is that many would do the same for me. I was too stubborn to let others, which made it difficult for them to show me how much they loved me. Love is a powerful energy that needs to be given and received and the knowledge of that perspective is the powerful gift Grandma Alice gave me with her final request.

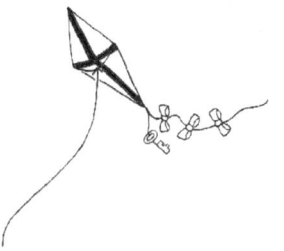

Chapter Four

Observe, Don't Absorb:
What They Think About You
Isn't Really About You

(The First Bridle String of Your Kite)

My first year of teaching, I was filled with excitement. I had been going to college two days a week while my children attended an at-home daycare so I could complete my degree. I had packed my schedule so heavily with my schoolwork and my young children's activities with friends and family to manifest this career. There were many early mornings and late nights working on papers and assignments and I was constantly juggling those oppressive deadlines with the list of things I needed to do for my family. Now all the stress was finally behind me, and I was so excited to be embarking on this new path. My original plan was to sub until I was able to find a permanent job, but then, in true small-town fashion, I heard about a great opportunity that led me to bump up my expectations. Toward the end of the summer, when a friend of mine dropped her daughter off for a playdate with Kelsie, she told me another mother in her daycare was interviewing for an English teacher at her school. By the next week I began the interview process, already anticipating the new possibilities available with an additional income in our family.

When I found out I got the position, I was ecstatic. The timing was perfect, as my younger child was starting kindergarten that year. When I saw the previous teacher had left the room all decorated with butterflies, I felt it was surely a sign of transformation. My new colleagues, who were seasoned teachers, were very kind and nurturing, and I had the most amazing group of students that I could have asked for. It was a blissful beginning to the career I had dreamed of since I was a child, lining up my dolls on the floor for the lesson of the day when I was five years old. Now in my early thirties it had finally become a reality and I could not wait to get started.

As the year progressed, I had one student I just could not seem to engage. He neglected to hand in work and seemed to be in my class only for the social interaction. Although I found him to be very gregarious and personable, I couldn't get him excited about the class work, despite my best efforts to be creative with lesson plans. My attempts at heart-to-heart conversations didn't work either; I just didn't have enough experience to come up with viable solutions and he didn't seem very receptive. His grade continued to slip, and by the time parent-teacher conferences came around he was failing and I was feeling defeated. I discussed the situation with a colleague and we came up with some ideas on how we could work together to help him since I felt responsible for his success.

On the day of the conferences, he and his family – mom, dad, and-younger sister crowded around my little table to get the latest update on his progress. I felt my heart rate pulsing at the base of my throat, while my student stared off at a spot on the wall behind me. I sheepishly shared his progress report – not a very time-consuming act since there was not much else to say other than he was currently failing to turn in any work. As I discussed my observations, I felt a sinking feeling in my stomach. Somehow, I couldn't seem to squelch the guilty feeling rustling around in my gut, and watching my student sink into his chair seemed to heighten my discomfort. Then his father asked if we could go into my classroom for some privacy. Ignoring the foreboding feeling that washed over me, I agreed and led the family into my room. It was then that the onslaught of name-calling and blame began.

I was immediately transported back to my youth and felt defensive and helpless. I felt that if I said anything he would just attack me further, so I stayed quiet. The barrage didn't stop as he continued to question me about why his son was failing. Attempts to mention the ideas I discussed with my colleague were unsuccessful, in part because I was so taken aback by how I was being disrespected and humiliated I couldn't remember what we decided would be the best measures to take to get him on track. His wife interrupted in an attempt to diffuse the tension, but he continued to confront me, saying things like, "How dare you say he is failing in front of his little sister? What were you thinking!?" As this was my first round of conferences, I had no precedent to draw on. Would parents be this rude to me for the rest of my career? The stress was accumulating in my body and my thoughts began to blur.

I was not one for confrontation and my self-preservation boundaries were not yet established so this interaction seemed particularly triggering. I just looked at my student and my heart sank. I figured if the father was yelling at me then at least his son was getting a break. He just kept saying, in many colorful ways, how little he thought of me as a teacher and asking a barrage of questions that became so personal and piercing, I was grateful he didn't give me time to answer. Needless to say, it wasn't a productive conversation, and I didn't feel like it was going to shift but I wasn't sure how to end this private conference. Finally, my colleague knocked on the door and I couldn't get across the room fast enough to open it. She must have heard the yelling – I suspect everyone within the confines of the building could. I wasn't given an opportunity to speak and I could feel the heat pulsing in my neck, which had turned red where the unspoken words were gathering in my throat. I had never prepared myself for the verbal lashing I had received. Somehow, the exchange had become an attack that was about me as a person, not just as a teacher.

After one glance, my colleague said, "It sounds as if this is something that should be handled at another time when tempers are not as high"; she then put her hand on my shoulder to guide me out the door to safety. I heard her suggest the family head out and it was then that I noticed my body was shaking. I became immediately aware of the sea of unfamiliar faces all focused on me. It was horrific to have those faces staring at me, and I wasn't sure how to regain my composure. At that moment I was feeling so many things all of which revolved around every insecurity I had as a new teacher and as a person in general. I felt so vulnerable standing in front of the group of unfamiliar faces, I was wishing there was a trap door somewhere so I could escape.

I believed that the verdict from the wide-eyed parents in the room was that I wasn't worthy to be their child's teacher either. I instantly created a whole story in my head of what each person must be thinking about me. I felt like an errant little child getting scolded for something I wasn't solely responsible for. I couldn't help but rerun the insults from this father in my head – and feel like they were being mirrored in the faces of those waiting in line. I was certain they all must have been silently agreeing with that angry parent.

My principal arrived moments later and asked me to come with him; then he politely told the next parents in line that I would be back in five minutes. I went into the safe confines of his office and recounted the events with as much clarity as I could without crying. I asked him how much of that I was supposed to take, and he turned to me and suggested I don't take any of that treatment, ever. That is when the idea was sparked, though I wouldn't realize it until much later.

I still had another hour of conferences and a line of eager parents who had witnessed the confrontation. If I had my choice, I would have just gone home; however, since that was not an option, I got some water and went back to my desk for the next meeting. The lingering aftermath of what had been said, and overheard, was like an elephant in the room. I was so self-conscious and worried about what those people were thinking that I could barely function. As it turned out, the rest of my interactions were very positive. I felt somewhat comforted that I only had one angry parent out of over one hundred students. Unfortunately, that is the only one I dwelled on. I had over twenty conferences that night and all were positive and amiable, but the one that lingered was the negative one and I just could not stop focusing on what was said. It seemed so personal and yet public as well.

That conference taught me a valuable lesson about how I digested unpleasant interactions and what they were actually there to show me. If I stayed in victim mode and absorbed any of the nasty accusations that man hurled at me, I probably would not have returned the next day to teach which would have robbed me of a twenty-year career! How ridiculous to give someone that much power. I wanted to defend myself and convince this father that I wasn't the monster he made me out to be. I also recognized that I was falling into old patterns of feeling insecure about myself. That father's words were not a true reflection of who I was. When I started to realize that I didn't need him to like me, I was able to release the guilty feelings I had swirling around in my head and refocus on what that exchange had taught me.

I believe that when we are interacting with people it is just an experience. We put the emotional and energetic charge on the interaction and create our version of events based on what we have learned by socialization or life experiences. Since we all see our circumstances through our own lens, there are bound to be variations in perception. When that student's father verbally attacked me, I was having flashbacks of being a helpless child getting yelled at by an authority figure. It was a trigger and I was completely activated. I was acutely aware of the angst I felt as a little girl, not knowing how to articulate my feelings in situations as they were unfolding. I was always taught to respect my elders and not to talk back, and I carried that belief with me well into adulthood. I had internalized so many feelings by staying silent over the years of my life. I justified this by telling myself that people didn't want to know what I was really feeling because expressing my feelings was somehow disrespectful. If I didn't agree or had a different point of view, I kept silent out of "respect" for others. Staying silent and absorbing this negativity was not honoring my feelings, which was an unhealthy manifestation of that advice. It was another skill I just seemed to adopt without realizing it… until that night.

As time passed and I had a few days to reflect on what happened, I remembered my principal saying that I didn't have to take any of the man's hateful words to heart. Not one bit of it had anything to do with me, really; he was just releasing pent-up emotions that I triggered when I told him his son was failing. However, in that moment, all I heard in his angry rant was how *I* was a failure in every aspect of my life.

I then began to reflect on my role as a teacher in a more objective way. I had tried to reach my student but at the end of the day, I couldn't force him to do his work. I had some limitations on how to make him successful because he wasn't participating. His father was reacting to that situation, not me.

I would continue to learn from this experience as my own

children got older. I realized how invested I was in their success and how personally I took their failures. This helped me understand where this parent may have been in his head. It also highlighted my trepidation about the meeting because he was the one student I couldn't seem to engage or inspire. I had such fantasies of being an amazing teacher and couldn't fathom failing to help even one of my students. What I found, years into my career, is that I am only a small part of a large team of teachers that impacts each student. I can only own my intentions and do my best, but in the end, it is not all my responsibility to make a student successful. That student is the main player on the team, and if he does not do any work the rest of us cannot do ours.

After that night, I never was able to talk with the angry father again. This was another lesson: oftentimes we will not have the chance to revisit a painful exchange with the other party to find closure. What I had to do was focus on how I was going to release those lingering feelings. Yes, I wanted to defend myself. I also wanted to redirect him and articulate all the reasons that what he was blurting out about me were not true. Instead, I had to recognize that he didn't know me any better than I knew him. I had to shift my focus to the people in my life who did know me and did not talk to me in such a derogatory manner. I do not need to "fix" the situation with the other person in order to release the emotions, and when I recognized that, I was able to take my power back from that angry father.

After several years of teaching, I thankfully realize that this was an isolated incident. I also became aware that what parents or students or even colleagues think of me really is none of my business. Worrying about what others think can feel important as I navigate my way through the world, but it really isn't. We all have layered life experiences that create the way we view the world and everyone in it. Someone yelling at me doesn't automatically mean it is about me; it is how they are choosing to express whatever is going on in their lives; but how I react does have everything to do with me. If it triggers me then I know there is work to be done. My awareness is that whenever I am giving too much energy to what people think of me, I am out of alignment with my true self. This experience also highlighted the reality that sometimes people will come into my life that don't like me, and I had to decide that I was ok with that. I have learned to take time and space to reflect and heal what shows up for me, which was a big shift in my perspective.

It takes a concentrated effort for me to shift from being triggered to being empowered, and I have let that become a more common response for me. I have learned to redirect my thinking to find it interesting…rather than just letting it go directly to my core as a certainty. That is not to say I am not interacting with people and learning each day, but I am not as quick to assume that only one point of view is my truth. There is a time for reflection in which I can honestly ask myself what, if any of this, is my responsibility? I can't just go through my daily experiences assuming that none of the energy exchange in any interaction is my responsibility, but it is imperative to get some clarity about what I am learning. I try to think about what I can do, and what I am willing to do to rectify the situation. I am also mindful when I am the one who triggers others with my words or actions. In each scenerio, I like to evaluate what other elements of the interaction may be impacting what is actually transpiring, for all involved and I am more likely to avoid going into victim mode or feeling defensive when I practice discernment to get clarity.

The exchange with the angry parent also highlighted another aspect of my personality. In the heat of the moment, I created a story in my head about everyone agreeing that I am not going to be an effective teacher. This was my own insecurity being shown to me so I could heal it. I am thankful it happened my first year, and as the years progressed, I was much more confident. Having that first exchange made me assess what kind of teacher I wanted to be. I could only control the intent and integrity that I poured into each lesson plan and interaction with students. The bonus is that I became much more contemplative not only in my professional life, but in all aspects of my daily practices with friends and family as well. I am making an effort to live my life being open to experiences and more a reflective observer, and not always an absorber.

What I have decided is that the various exchanges with other people is to teach, learn, or hold space for my own spiritual growth. Clarity doesn't always happen in the moment, especially if my emotions start getting activated, but it doesn't take as long to process because I have the awareness that I can take control of my own actions and words and step back to look at the elements affecting the exchange. I have to rely on the tools that I have accumulated in my spiritual practice, and my exploration of myself at retreats and various classes with mentors. I trust myself to discern what I am culpable for. It was easier for me to fall into old patterns of letting what others think about me be an area of concern for me to fix or somehow make better. What I learned is that other people and their opinions are not necessarily in alignment with me or my intentions. This helped me see that I don't need to take what is said about me to heart. While I would have liked to turn the conversation around or even to defend myself by rattling off how the nuances of my degree qualify me to be his son's teacher, it really wasn't necessary. In fact, it probably would have further incited his anger. What I decided is that spending the time to defend my character to him, or anyone I barely know, is not where I want to put my energy.

I need to be cognizant of what stories I am creating in my head about my self-worth as well. I am free to discern what is in my best interest and hold space, but I do not let the negativity and anger from someone else morph into my truth. If a comment or situation is out of alignment for me, I am strong enough to have compassion and empathy but also the clarity to learn or leave for my highest good. While the experience wasn't pleasant, it was powerful and has encouraged me to practice a new way of interpreting conflict, rather than letting what other people think of me have a detrimental effect on who I strive to be each day.

This is a constant practice of reflection and not taking things people say personally. When you are standing in your power and using your voice, it connects to the other parts of your kite. There are two strings that attach to the bridle of a kite. One comes from the spine of the kite, which is choosing to make yourself and your feelings a priority in your life. The other string comes from the horizontal bar, which is allowing yourself to be loved and facing your fears confidently, knowing that you will be successful. When you combine these two skills, you are reflecting on situations with a discernment about what you choose to observe so you are empowered, rather than activating a defense mechanism that no longer serves you.

If you do not feel uplifted or inspired by the people you are with, then you have the power to change any or all aspects of the situation. Take the time and use your energy to decide if what you are experiencing is to teach, learn or hold space for your own spiritual growth and then use your skills to act in your best interest. I like to repeat mantras to help me get out of a negative or old pattern of reacting to shift my mindset so I can move forward.

Observation is the first bridle string of your kite. It is developed after you are clear on who you are and are open to receiving love from others. Every person has their own perspective and stories they are reacting to as they go through their day. Just because someone has an opinion and lashes out it doesn't automatically mean that you are the cause of the interaction. Be mindful and take responsibility if it is yours. Be aware of your boundaries and your reactions. Do your best to analyze what you are experiencing and clear whatever is yours so you can eliminate triggers in the future. We are learning every day – and raising or lowering our energetic vibration with each interaction – so be mindful and take responsibility for your own healing. Remember, what others think about you isn't about you, so you can observe and not absorb!

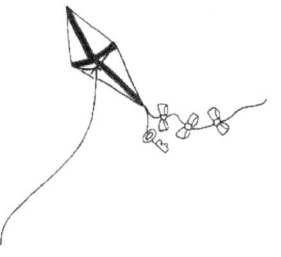

Chapter Five

Find Your Voice and Use It
(The Second String on the Bridle of Your Kite)

I was extroverted as a little girl and making new friends was rather easy for me because I loved being around people. My dad likes to tell me how excitedly I would jump in my crib and squeal when I saw him enter to pick me up in the morning. His reaction to my happiness made me even happier. As I started school, my family moved several times and I was often the new kid. I embraced it as an adventure in my youth; however, as I grew up and felt more attached to friends and having a home to go to and I started to really dislike the lack of continuity in my routine. Somehow it became more difficult to move, again and again. I found that I wasn't as extroverted or excited by the new school and people I was forced to engage with. I found myself trying to blend in and stay in the background because I didn't like being new and not having a history with the other students. I also became aware of cliques and found it harder to navigate friendships. I wasn't as open because I was learning how to avoid standing out. I'm not sure when I stopped genuinely expressing my feelings, but it was an inevitable transition as I tried to blend into my new surroundings and new house and new routine in a new town. It was a lot to juggle, and I became much less enthusiastic about it.

Somewhere along my journey, I stopped expressing my true inner thoughts. I didn't want to be too vulnerable with new people, and the risk of criticism or not fitting in became more of a priority than my happiness. By my teenage years I often found myself apologizing in virtually every conversation. "Sorry" became a complete sentence for me. It was an instant response and then when I was told I didn't need to apologize, I apologized again. Controlled by fear and a high sensitivity to other's feelings, I learned to stay quiet and avoid what I perceived as conflict which transmuted into other areas of my life. I felt like any verbal altercation was to be avoided because I didn't know how to process anger or discontent very well, especially when it wasn't mine. Part of my issue was how sensitive I was to the energy of literally everyone around me. If I could feel tensions rising or energy shifting within others, I would try to balance out the energy by absorbing what I could. I wanted others to be happy and did my best with what tools I had, but using my voice was not one of the skills I had developed. The years of placating others to avoid conflict continued … until my daughter's graduation party.

I had started attending an advanced meditation class that met one weekend a month for a year. It was a group of six other women that all were shifting and learning about more than meditation. We often discussed what issues had come up for us and offered advice or comfort after each person shared. When it came time for me to share, I mentioned that we were remodeling our kitchen for my daughter's graduation party. I was ridiculously excited to get a farmhouse sink so I no longer had to wrestle with the two small sides of the outdated sink I had. Dealing with splashing water on me and the floor every time I washed the frying pan that was too big to fit in the divided sink would finally be over. Once the decisions were made, the anticipation began, with my family eating out for two weeks until the construction was completed.

The construction crew had packed up their tools and I was able to see the new modifications all complete, without a mess. The new counter and marble on the island gave the room a new warmth. I made my way to the sink to marvel at all the space I had, and that is when I noticed a large gouge in the bottom by the drain. I blew away the shavings and ran my nail over the scratch and realized that it was really deep. I was very disappointed to say the least. I had waited for weeks to have my kitchen back in working order; and it was already ruined before I even got to run the water. I justified that the sink couldn't be new forever and I figured I could just let it go, but deep down inside I was really upset.

I went to bed thinking about how deep the scratch was and how it would always be there. I just wanted my sink to be perfect for my daughter's graduation and I thought about the damage the whole twenty-minute ride into town for my meditation class the next morning. Knowing about the renovations, my group members asked how the kitchen turned out. I tried to mention all of the elements of the renovation that I was thrilled about – the new handles on the cupboards, the countertops, and the way the kitchen felt so much bigger… and then the image of the deep groove in the bottom that ruined my brand-new sink permeated my thoughts. I wasn't going to say anything, but I just couldn't stop thinking about how dissatisfied I was. I could feel my neck getting red with anxiety and I wondered whether I should share my disappointment. In a split-second decision, I figured this would be a safe place to air my grievances, so I recounted the discovery of the scratch in the sink. I immediately regretted my decision as each member of the group seemed to be emotionally triggered by the incident.

I started to get an onslaught of advice from every member of the group in unison. I could feel their anger and frustration in addition to my own and started to feel self-conscious. The energy of the room had shifted, and I was embarrassed that I was the reason. Being the center of attention was a familiar feeling since I moved so much growing up, but it was still very uncomfortable. In a knee-jerk reaction I started to downplay the scratch, but I was interrupted. Mercifully, they all took turns this time so I could actually hear what was being said. Individually each member began ruthlessly coaching me and telling me that I needed to tell the manager of the construction crew that I wasn't satisfied. I stifled my feelings and tried to rationalize how silly it was to get upset about a sink, but the lump in my throat kept forcing me to talk. I even apologized for taking so much time out of our meditation class to listen to me complain.

All the comments had the same undercurrent: "Just tell

them to replace it. No big deal." As I played each suggested scenario in my head of how to tell the construction crew, I realized I was getting really upset; nausea forced its way into a lump in my throat. "No, it is okay, it was bound to get scratched eventually," I rationalized. But my group members kept hounding me, imitating me as they replayed the conversations from the previous month's meeting in anticipation of the remodel. This was a crossroads; I would never live it down if I just relied on my old strategy of not speaking up. The advice continued despite my attempts to shift the conversation. Encouragement masked as ultimatums of what I needed to say continued. I needed to use my voice and I wasn't sure how this was going to turn out. I knew they would ask next month how it went, and I couldn't just ignore my feelings this time. Too many people were invested in how this turned out. I had never really stood up for myself and thinking about whose advice I was going to take made my body start to sweat.

"I can just have a scratched sink and be grateful for the other improvements that we invested in," I said meekly, which just fanned the flames.

"It is your brand-new sink," one said. "Yeah," said another, "Tell them you're pissed!"

I wanted it to be someone else's turn to share; I felt as though I had somehow sparked everyone's anger and frustration in the room. Then the fear and anxiety of a potential confrontation with the construction manager bubbled up and I started to cry. Not a full-on bellow, but I couldn't manage to stop the tears from rolling down my cheeks as the group blurted out their suggestions with a few expletives thrown in. I just wanted to crawl in a hole and take back the brief moment of bravery that made me decide to share. After praying silently for it all to stop, I managed to say, "It's fine, please, will someone else start sharing," but it fell on deaf ears. Our facilitator took over the conversation and finally quelled the stream of advice.

I was asked to reflect about what emotions were coming up for me and I drew a blank. I didn't really understand why this was turning into such a big deal. I rationalized that it wasn't worth upsetting everyone here or anyone on the remodeling crew. I really didn't need to cause such a stir over a scratch, and my daughter's graduation certainly wouldn't be ruined by such a minute detail. Clearly, none of our guests would be looking in the bottom of the sink.

But as I was continuously prompted by our facilitator to answer his reflection inquiries, I finally realized that this was a pattern for me. My whole life I had stuffed feelings and kept silent to placate the people around me, especially in unfamiliar situations. This was an opportunity for me to shift this old pattern and use my voice to express my true feelings. For me, using my voice was associated with making people uncomfortable or irascible; it just didn't seem worth it since I could always feel that too. I had conditioned myself to believe that it was just easier for me to sort it out on my own and not involve anyone else, which is why I was reticent to tell my group what I was feeling. I had convinced myself that the idea of not sharing protected me from the emotions that I was having with the meditation group staring at me, but I was starting to realize that this was not a healthy life strategy. In reality, they were all just encouraging me to stretch a little, even if it was uncomfortable for me. It was about finding my voice and using it, which was not a tool I employed until I had this experience.

What I learned is that it is okay for me to own my feelings and express them. How I got this far in my life without having the realization escaped me, but I needed to start to shift how I perceived conflict. Yes, my strategies had seemed to work up to this point – just say sorry to placate others and potentially end any unpleasantness I was feeling – however, that was not the adult way to interact with others. I had to realize that it was not my responsibility to make others feel better at the expense of being dishonest and not owning my feelings.

If I was responsible for how I feel, then it was certainly true for others as well. My facilitator pointed out that I can't make anyone else feel anything, good or bad – we are all responsible for our own reactions and feelings. I knew I had heard that before, but when he said it that day, it resonated with me. I actually took in the gravity of those words and what they meant. It wasn't just for the kitchen to look amazing during my daughter's graduation party; it was a turning point for me in communicating my feelings. Denying how I feel about events in my life stifles my voice. If I just address my own energy and let everyone else take responsibility for their own, then I don't drain my reserves trying to make people feel a certain way. The realization that I can't shift what other people are feeling, only my own thoughts and reactions, was a powerful tool for me.

Refusing to communicate what I was feeling would continue to result in stuffed emotions popping up, just as they had in class. The group encouraged me to take a chance and talk to the construction company and tell them about the damaged sink. As the discussion progressed, their tone became much more gentle and genuine – they all knew this was a challenge for me and their advice turned to compassion and encouragement, with a little less vitriol.

While I was driving home, I replayed all the varied scenarios and tried to convince myself that I could do it. I rehearsed what I would say as I conjured up an air of confidence in the faux conversation rattling through my head. My body was trembling as I dialed the number. I tried to take a deep breath, but I was so nervous, my lungs only seemed to be functioning at a third of their normal capacity. This call was about so much more than a scratch in a new sink or my daughter's graduation party. I could feel the shift of a lifelong pattern I had developed, and I had myself so worked up that I barely noticed someone had answered. I started with what I loved but I knew it was just a tactic to delay what I really needed to say; there was no turning back. I almost ended the conversation, but the advice from my group started to replay in my head and I knew I needed to stand in my power and stop holding on to the pattern of worrying about everyone else at the expense of my own well-being. I took a sip of water and mentioned the concern I had with the deep scratch in the new sink. I acknowledged that it was most likely an accident, but I was really disappointed that it was so damaged before I actually used it.

To my surprise, the man was sorry for the incident and

replaced the sink the next day, so anticlimactic after all the emotions that were stirred in me and the friends in my meditation group. The blessing was that I had finally given myself permission to speak my truth. It never occurred to me that the Earth would still rotate on its axis if I told anyone when I was disappointed, frustrated, or even angry. I had spent so many years putting other people first and always being available to help them that I neglected myself or just apologized if I had any uncomfortable thoughts or ideas about a situation.

I was also able to shift old beliefs about what conflict is. Not all interaction within discrepant situations is about conflict. Sometimes, it is an opportunity for defining and setting boundaries and standing in your personal power. I had to define my limits and stop apologizing for my point of view. I also had to stop lying to myself and others about how I was feeling in any given situation. It was a self-sabotaging behavior that was out of alignment for me. Now I own my feelings and share them; and let others do the same. I now know that I can find joy in my relationships and friendships and be more genuine and honest about my feelings.

This is the string connecting the bridle of my kite – the string that links the horizontal bar of the kite to the vertical bar – and it works in tandem with choosing yourself and not worrying about what others think. It is imperative to develop your own truth and express it with your voice. It doesn't need to be loud or angry, it can be gentle and firm, like this part of your kite. It took a lot of courage, but once I found my voice, I realized how powerful it is. It still takes time for me to be in a place where I will take the energy to speak up for myself, but I do it more and more with less anxiety. What I have found is that communicating my true feelings is an important part of being my authentic self, which is why it is such an integral part of the kite.

When I don't use my voice, I am letting other people choose for me which is not an empowered way to live. When I do use it, I find that people are genuinely responsive to my feelings and do find a solution without conflict, which shattered my previous assumptions. The energy I was using to make sure everyone else was okay is now refocused on me and my happiness. I am living much more authentically and encouraging those around me to do the same. Using your voice to express how you are truly feeling is an important part of communicating. It takes practice to express yourself with love and kindness, and it can be difficult to integrate this new skill if it does not come naturally to you, but you can do it. The important part to remember is that you are worthy of having your feelings honored. It is also vital to achieving balance, both internally and in our communications with others. Empowering yourself to use your voice can be an amazing gift for you – even better than a new sink!

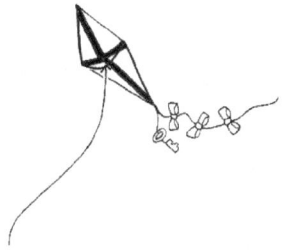

Chapter Six

Finding Your Tribe
(Choose Your Kite Fabric and Trim It)

eople come into our lives for a reason, a season, or a lifetime. No matter how long they stick around, your time together can have a lifelong impact, especially when the connection is deep. Janet was someone who taught me how to conscientiously connect with people and how important it is to really choose who I spend time with. We have an annual retreat each year at our church, and after a few years some of us had become "regulars." It was a wonderful time of bonding, sharing, relaxing, crafting, and visiting that only a weekend away from our other responsibilities afforded. There was always time for reflection and sharing after each break-out session, and I got to see a more intimate side of the people there which sparked a deeper friendship that grew throughout the years. There were always small groups within the main group; and everyone seemed to find their niche and enjoy the time with new friends and soul sisters.

Janet was one of those friends. Open-hearted and thoughtful, she also had a very playful personality and a magical way of making me feel heard and seen. When we first talked it was very unsettling, but that was the beauty of our interaction. Those uncomfortable moments are the ones that seem to have the most potential for growth, and meeting Janet was definitely one of those moments for me. On our first retreat together, we had broken into small groups for a scripture-based discussion about what it means to be vulnerable. Many of us had a hard time really pinpointing the nuances of that emotion in a verbally coherent way. In our small group we all defined vulnerability with subtle differences.

One person in our group stated that it depends on the situation, only to be countered by another who contended that it depends on who you are with. I had never really pondered how or when I felt vulnerable, so when it was my turn to comment I wasn't sure what to say. I felt like the answers others had given applied to me at one point or another, but I wasn't ready to narrow it down to one specific reason. As I was talking, I noticed that Janet was looking very intently in my eyes, like she was hanging on every word. It was the perfect storm for me to be exploring the concept of vulnerability. I felt so exposed!

I looked at others in the group to get some reprieve and shift my focus, but I could always feel her looking at me, listening. When I did return to her, her soft eyes were very intently locked on mine. It felt very unsettling. I heard myself stumbling over my words and finding it almost invasive to have her making such consistent eye-contact while I explored my feelings. I was thankful for the reprieve when it was time to join our small circles together into one and share our insights.

Janet assumed the role of group spokesperson and relayed what we had discussed. She individually recounted what each person said; then, when she discussed what I said, she looked right into my eyes once again. When I averted my gaze to look around the room, she stopped talking. Aware of the awkward silence, I looked back at Janet. She locked eyes with me and continued and then winked at me when she had finished sharing what I had said. I'm not sure what made it so uncomfortable when she looked directly at me, but my body seemed to have a visceral reaction and I found myself looking away several times. Then I just tried to avoid her altogether because it was too much for me to process. I wasn't sure why it bothered me so much and I needed time to figure out what feelings were emerging.

As I watched Janet, I noticed that she made a concerted effort to look into the eyes of whomever was speaking or listening to during the retreat. She wasn't staring; it was more personal. She was acknowledging a soul connection and was gently smiling and nodding as an active listener. Surely, I had looked at a person's face to catch their expressions, but I realized that I didn't really focus on a person's eyes when I talked to them - certainly not as long as Janet seemed accustomed to. It was a level of intimacy – intense and almost otherworldly – that I had never engaged in, even with my friends.

At first, I let that uncomfortable feeling of being so open and unable to break eye contact squelch my enjoyment of engaging with her. And, as it turned out, I wasn't the only one.

That night, my roommate commented on how unsettling it was to have Janet be so intently looking into her eyes, which she considered the window to her soul. Intrigued, I asked Janet why she held someone's eyes in that way when speaking with them. She had a ready answer about how important it is to her that one be seen, not just heard.

"I just hate it when I am talking," she said, "and the person is staring at their phone or looking away because it feels like they are not really listening to me, so I make an effort not to let people feel that way when they are talking to me."

As the retreat continued, I saw how right she was. I realized I had a tendency to look away, especially if I was feeling particularly vulnerable. Janet was trying to tell me that she saw me and didn't feel the need to look away. It was her version of a hug and unlimited support no matter what I was feeling which was difficult to get used to.

I spent some time journaling and really contemplating what I thought about interacting with people that way. Then, in our afternoon circle, we had our chance to be completely exposed and look into each other's eyes the "Janet way."

At each retreat, we sang a song, "How Could Anyone"[1] by Alaskan singer/songwriter Libby Roderick. It became an anthem of connection that we sang every year before lunch on the second day. We joked about how we loathed the dreaded circle

---

[1] Roderick, Words and m Libby. 1990. "How Could Anyone?" Turtle Island Records, Anchorage Alaska. www.libbyroderick.com libbyroderick@gmail.com Lyrics reprinted with permission.

where we had to get through the song because it made us so emotionally exposed, with tears flowing unchecked. But we loved it too, as well as all the hugs that followed this exercise, which seemed to solidify the deep friendships among the re-treaters. The lyrics are poignant in their simplicity – just four questions gently repeated over and over:

> *How could anyone ever tell you, you were anything less than beautiful?*
>
> *How could anyone ever tell you, you were less than whole?*
>
> *How could anyone fail to notice that your loving is a miracle*
>
> *How deeply you're connected to my soul?*

We always began the activity with our hands clasped, sing-ing along with conviction and joy while the Libby Roderick CD played in the background. Once the music started, it wasn't hard to follow along with the lyrics; however, this be-came more difficult to do as we repeated the song and activated our emotions – and we saw those emotions reflected on each other's faces. How could we believe we aren't beautiful? There are so many external elements from the internet or media that influence our low self-esteem, and very few that seem to sup-port the concept of true beauty. As women we have so much to offer the world with our compassion, creativity, and empa-thetic hearts and so many undefinable ways to shine our light – and yet we downplay the unique beauty in ourselves. As we sang, the realization that we are whole and complete just as we are became our new perspective.

Our ability to love and be vulnerable while we conquer our fears truly is a testament to our power to form loving bonds with one another. As the song repeated and our vulnerability became more intense, we would put our arms on each other's shoulders which tightened our circle. This made it easier to see each other's eyes. Our chorus of twenty women always started off strong, but as each woman started to reflect on the words and became overwhelmed with unescapable emotion, her lips would quiver and the sound would falter. Making eye contact became more difficult as the mascara-laced tears trailed down each other's faces. As we grappled with the intensity of our emotions, it was much easier to look at the floor or at someone's legs rather than let them see into your soul. As we finished the final verse, the mighty chorus was down to two or three meek voices, drowned out by the incessant sniffles. Looking into each other's eyes was a whole new level of connection, and it was a deep recognition of our own beauty and love that was emanating from each teary-eyed person in the circle.

We stayed interlocked in our circle long after the CD stopped, letting the emotions rack through our bodies until we all took a big collective breath and released them through the exhale. We stood together in silence before we broke out of our circle, then enveloped one another in individual hugs before going to lunch to reflect and discuss what came up for us.

Janet often had the most thought-provoking reflections and discussion-starters. She was great at putting the triggered emotions into perspective, interjecting humor and levity in such a way that we left lunch in tears of laughter as we headed into our afternoon activities. She loved the eye-contact and intensity of the activity; it was her favorite song to sing every year and she was the master of connecting to each woman's soul with her intimate eye-contact. It was piercing and penetrating, and it was done with such gentleness and compassion; it became a confirmation that we do see the beauty in each other and there is no need to look away.

One year, as the annual retreat approached, we learned that Janet was battling an aggressive form of cancer and wouldn't be able to join us. Stunned and saddened by the news, we made a somber trip to her house to hold a mini retreat just for her. While gathering my things I decided to pack my t-shirt with the lyrics of Libby Roderick's song. I had purchased it after the first retreat and wore it often to our monthly mothers' group. Whenever Janet saw me wearing it, she made a point to stop me, playfully pull it away from my waist, and read the lyrics aloud while looking into my eyes. When she was done, she would wink and thank me for the reminder before giving me a hug. It always made me laugh, and I loved her hugs. I decided that I would give her the shirt as a gift from all of us.

That night, despite our sorrow, we were able to laugh as we took turns regaling Janet with stories and fun memories from previous retreats. Janet was so weak she couldn't even open the gift bag, so I pulled out the t-shirt and gently laid it by her hand. Her eyes were closed most of the time, but we knew from her weak smile that she was participating in her own way. As our visit was winding down, our pastor suggested we sing what had become the anthem of our women's retreats. Suddenly, Janet opened her eyes and tried to lift her head.

Shocked at her burst of energy, several of us stuffed many pillows behind her so she could sit up. As we gathered in a circle around her bed and continued to sing to her, she fumbled around her sheets and found the T-shirt we had given her earlier in the evening, gently enclosing her fingers around it.

As we put our arms on each other's shoulders and began to sway side to side, I watched with my heart in my throat as Janet held the t-shirt up as high as she could. It was her effort to sing with us in her weakened state. Janet made the conscious effort to look into each of our eyes as she clutched the shirt in the air. I was tempted to look down, but I was so thankful that I found the courage to look into her eyes. They were glistening with unshed tears and when she winked at me; I smiled and winked back. As I felt the tear trail down my cheek, I realized we were saying our final goodbye. It was heart-wrenching and beautiful. I knew I was really seeing into her soul, and it was the last time I would have the opportunity to be held in her eyes – and her heart.

She continued around the circle to connect with each of us until her husband entered the room, signaling that our visit had come to an end. We all gathered around her in one last group hug, and Janet continued to hold the shirt up and wave it as we reluctantly filed out of her room. As I looked back one more time, I saw that her husband was reading over the lyrics on the shirt. With a gentle smile, he gave her a kiss on the forehead and fluffed her pillows as we headed to the church van, with our hearts heavy with grief. Watching Janet's final gesture of holding up the shirt touched us so deeply, evoking emotions we couldn't articulate and certainly would never forget.

Janet transitioned two days later. At her funeral, her husband told me that she was still holding the shirt when she passed away. Knowing how much she loved it, he had put it in her hand when she was laid in her coffin. It was a touching symbol of our soul connection and I am deeply moved that she has the shirt with her for eternity.

A few weeks later the retreat rolled around. We decided to leave a candle burning on Janet's empty chair during the entire weekend so she could be with us. She was literally shining her light in our circle. It was a powerful reflection for us to question what is really important in our lives. Why are we so willing to listen to the criticism from others instead of realizing the power of love and our deep connection to one another? When it came to Janet's final moments, no one cared if we had mascara dripping down our cheeks or what we were wearing. That moment was simply a reflection of who we are as people and what it means to be complete, even in our imperfection. In her final moments, when all of the worldly concerns no longer took precedence, Janet showed me how powerful it is to really look into someone's eyes and have them simultaneously look back and feel that intense, loving and timeless connection. It gave me permission to let the doubts and insecurities I have about being seen by others go. It is not serving me at all to believe that I am anything less than beautiful, complete, and worthy of love. It was a life-changing shift that continues to impact my interactions with people every day.

I learned from this experience to be mindful of the people I spend time with, feel safe with, and trust to really see me. It is imperative to find people who lift you up and support you and let go of those who do not. This is the building of your tribe, and you must do it with intention and care. It may feel lonely at first, and releasing the emotional weight of unnecessary criticism from people around you is a huge step toward living authentically. You know who I am referring to: the ones who are not really listening to you or seeing deeply into your soul. They are too focused on what is going wrong in their lives and who is making them feel bad or incomplete in some way. Nothing is ever right. These people are perpetually negative, and they drain me instantly. This is not to say that I do not have compassion or empathy for those in pain, but I must also care for myself and recognize that some people aren't going to grow or shift out of that victim mindset. I understand that we can all dip into those feelings periodically and need support. However, when it is perpetual and the person is just repeating the story to whomever will listen without trying to shift it, it may be an indication that I am not the one that will be able to help no matter how hard I try. If I feel drained in their company constantly, or exhausted when I leave them, that is my sign that I need to gently release myself from the situation to maintain my own mental health and energy.

Choose to be with people that really see you and embrace who you are wherever you are in your journey. We all have shadows, fears, insecurities, responsibilities, and we also all have dreams and compassion and love to share. We do want to be seen and heard, as Janet pointed out. I am not sure I can master the gaze at the level she did, but I do see the integrity behind her decision. It is a comfort to know that although I initially felt raw and exposed, there came a time when I felt really safe with Janet. The vulnerability and intensity of eye contact illustrates a connection that is more than a moment and more than a look. That was my awareness of the insecurity that I had of being seen. It was a powerful and loving way to eradicate those self-imposed boundaries.

Human connection is a searing reminder of the powerful and magnetic light that we all emit from our souls. It is your light that draws people to you, and if you are brave enough to let it shine, it can engulf those around you in a beautiful way. I trusted Janet to see all of me and I knew that she was honest with me as well. That's how the friendship grew and we became soul sisters. When I had a problem or concern, she would listen just as intently as when I had good news or excitement to share. She was all in and engaged no matter what topic we were discussing. It was so empowering to be that honest with someone. I am not sure there are many that I let get that close to me, but in this instance, quantity can't replace quality. Your inner circle doesn't have to be big to be impactful. The importance of being in a tribe is that you can be vulnerable, and you can also be the one to encourage others. You want it to be an even exchange over time.

I want to be with people that have worked through some of their layers and are showing up each day. I am no longer willing to integrate other people's fears into my list of aspirations. Those people are the ones shouting advice from the sidelines or hiding back in the house when I am going for it and living my most authentic, empowered life. Be with the Janets of the world who will encourage you and see past your human struggles into the love of your soul and support your growth.

These friends will aid you on your life journey and will depend on you to do that for them. The key is to have someone that is authentic and truthful with their gifts as well as their struggles. Find someone who will also call you out when you are not aligned; the honesty is refreshing and will help you continue to grow.

Search to find those people who will heal, laugh, cry, listen, share, celebrate and encourage you, and embrace all of who you are – those who challenge you to see the world from multiple perspectives, beyond worldly concerns, and help you refocus where you are putting your energy. They are authentic and true to their beliefs and walk their talk. They also open up to you and trust you to do the same for them. That is what it means to surround yourself with people for your highest good. That is why it is imperative to choose your fabric wisely.

The quality of fabric is important in this kite metaphor. It must be neatly trimmed around the frame of your kite so it can fly with ease. It may be nice to have extra fabric or people, but it will impede the successful flight of your kite. Sometimes it is necessary to release people that are no longer aligned with your new vision or energy level. It can be sad or painful at times because as humans we are conditioned to believe that being alone is problematic. What I have found however is that you can be with people and still be lonely. It is the mindset you feel yourself slipping into when you are around individual people that you want to be mindful of. That is how you know if you are with high-vibrating people who are more aligned with where you are at the time. If there is no connection, respect, or trust then it is not necessary to hang on just for the sake of not being alone. Release the extraneous people, or fabric, so you can have a strong tribe that makes your life much more complete.

I have had people release me too and I tortured myself wondering what I did or how I could have fixed the situation. The reality is that our exchange was here to teach me or mirror for me what has been completed or is necessary to help foster learning. I don't need to try to replay what has been done. I trust that I am divinely guided and protected and that new people will come in and the cycle will continue. The people who remain will empower you to be the best version of your loving self and all of the changes will make sense. At some point, you will realize that the changes are worth those uncomfortable feelings that are elicited while your growth and expansion transpire and your relationships shift.

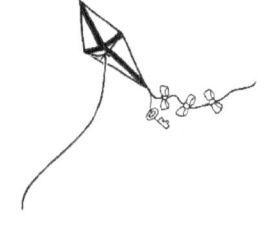

Chapter Seven

Trust With an Open Heart
(The String of Your Kite)

L earning to trust myself after years of self-abuse and sabotage was an uphill battle. I had a lot of strategies that were ineffective, yet I relied on them and kept unintentionally repeating unhealthy patterns. I trained myself to internalize fears and got in the habit of stuffing feelings. I had become so accustomed to doing that by the time I was in my forties it wasn't even a conscious decision. What I learned however is that there is no healthy way to stuff anything. It is like trying to hold a beach ball under water – eventually something shifts, and it pops up to the surface.

I didn't like to share some of those shadows and fears that lurked within me, and I let them manifest as fear that wasn't always rational. Trust, like everything else has layers; not only trusting others but trusting in myself is imperative, though it was not an overnight success for me. I spent so much time looking outside of myself and now had to learn how to look within, without a critical eye. I tend to live in the gray area of life where my thoughts spin on a hamster wheel, especially if emotions are triggered. It took a lot of time and energy for me to pinpoint the core of my answers with any clarity because I let them spin around in my head. What I learned from Thor, however, is that I have to get into my heart and out of fear if I am going to really engage in a life that is full of so much love. My epiphany started on a sunny fall day in a horse pasture out in the countryside of Minnesota for a women's retreat. I was with some of my best friends, all horse lovers, and their enthusiasm was contagious. We went around the circle to introduce ourselves and share why we decided to come to the retreat. I was excited, but I think I was the only one that was not inherently a horse-lover.

When it was my turn to talk, I confessed my feelings: "Well, I am scared to death of horses, and I want to get over my fear." My friend looked incredulously at me and laughed, "What the hell are you doing at a horse retreat if you're scared of horses?" which made everyone else laugh. It was a fair question, and as I looked over the fence at the various horses grazing, I pondered it as well. I had been so enthusiastic when I signed up from the comfort of my desk at home. My daughter had a horse named Lucy that she loved, and I really wanted to get over my fear of horses so I could enjoy being with her without all the nervous tension I seemed to initiate when I was around them both in the pasture. Now that I was actually here, breathing in the sweet grass from the neighboring meadow, I wasn't feeling the same confidence or excitement about my choice. I kept thinking that these horses are a lot more majestic when driving past them on the way to the farm. They seemed to be so much bigger and more intimidating to me less than one hundred feet away with no car to hide in, and I wasn't sure how to release my fears.

As the others in the group continued introducing themselves, I kept shifting in my seat silently praying that none of the horses would get the urge to jump over the meager fence that separated us. I had nervous energy surging through my body and a ball of tension nestled in my stomach, but I was determined to do this. I was with some of the most gentle-hearted women I have ever met in my life, and I knew I was supported. I secretly kept wishing we engaged in another activity together, but I knew this was going to be worth it if I conquered my fear. Indeed, that weekend would change my life in the most magical way.

As the golden hour of day one descended upon us, we were all encouraged to go to the fence and feed the herd of horses. I watched as the other women gleefully extended their hands with carrots to entice the horses to engage with us. I reached out my hand with the longest carrot I could find in the bucket and held it at the farthest distance in front of me. When the horse came closer to the fence, I instinctively dropped the carrot just as she began to nibble on the end. I felt bad that she had to lean down to get it off the ground, but my fear had kicked in and having her eat out of my hand was just too intimidating. I was not off to a great start, and I went to bed with a faint air of failure surrounding me and wondering what the rest of the retreat had in store.

I had a renewed vigor on day two. The other women tried to encourage me to share in their love of horses and I latched on to their excitement when it was my turn to lead the horse in a figure eight. I could barely move my feet across the corral from the safety of the group. The idea of having this huge animal so close to me made my knees weak. My heart was beating ridiculously fast considering the slow pace I used when I headed over to the trainer for my turn. I tried positive self-talk to quell the errant thoughts racing through my head at a frantic pace. I had been repeatedly reminded in the past that a horse can sense my fear, but I really couldn't make myself feel calm. In my agitated state, a beautiful golden horse nestled up to my side and swished her blonde tail across my shoulders as I leaned over to gather up her reins. I took the reins in my hand and started to walk on the desired path. When the slack from the reins had been tightened, I looked back at her and saw that she had completely extended her neck. I had a disturbing vision of dragging this poor horse by her mouth the whole way around the arena and felt a little disheartened. I wasn't really sure how to proceed since I didn't want to hurt her and I wasn't sure why she stopped. I was also acutely aware of how intimidating being in charge of this huge animal was and I felt my stomach roll with anxiety. Then, drawing from my parenting skills and in the sweetest voice I could conjure, I tried to encourage the horse, saying "Come on, it's okay." I wasn't sure that either of us was convinced, but she took a step toward me and I felt the tension in the reins relax. I took a deep breath, and we continued our walk.

I stood at the farthest reaches of her reins and sheepishly attempted to lead her in her corral. My first lap was a dilapidated oval, as I was too afraid to lean into her to make her cross over half-way through to make the figure eight. Her soft brown eyes looked down on me, her golden lashes were just above my head and when I looked up and made eye contact, I felt a little more comfortable and started to walk closer to her. I was acutely aware of her hooves hitting the soft dirt below us and tried to take larger steps to keep up with her without getting in her way. She actually moved on the desired path without me leading her and I was relieved that she took control of the situation. My resolve to lead her was not as potent as I was anticipating it would be before I engaged with this activity, and I was comforted that she knew the way.

Our evening group discussion was eye-opening. When the facilitator asked me to reflect on what I'd experienced, I explained that I felt a little more comfortable with the horse at my side but hadn't really taken control. I let her do it. I realized after some contemplation and lively discussion that this is one of my layers of trust that needed to be peeled away. When I don't trust myself to do something, I let other more confident people take over. I had become a person that didn't trust myself to lead the horse, and that was an insight into how I led my everyday life. I let my siblings, parents, friends and eventually my husband just handle details that they seemed confident doing. I didn't really force myself to learn how to navigate on my own if I knew someone else who liked to take charge, would.

As I journaled that night, I realized that this was a pattern for me. It was a way to dim my light and shy away from taking authority in situations where I lacked confidence or didn't know the outcome. It was all rooted in the insecurity and self-doubt rattling around in my head.

Where and why I started to think that was a good way to live was traced back to my childhood. Being the youngest, I determined that I needed to go with the flow, but that attitude over time caused me to become a spectator in my own life in many situations. I let others make decisions that I just went along with, without consciously thinking about how I actually felt. It occurred to me at that moment that I very rarely considered how I felt about the activities I participated in. I just went with the flow of others. Upon deeper reflection, I discovered that this permeated much of my daily life and I vowed to make changes when I got home.

I went into day three feeling a little more relaxed and amazed that a horse had helped me unearth a shadow aspect of my personality. I had a new perspective about the majesty of these animals, but I hadn't quite conquered my fear of them yet and the retreat was almost over. That was the day that Thor changed my ability to trust in myself. I was standing in the chilled arena on the last morning of the retreat, with soft dirt caking the boots I had borrowed from my daughter. I had to remind myself of the goal to heal my fear so I could share her love for her horse. I had set out to do this for her, but as the weekend progressed, I realized it was really about me. Day three had a new more invigorating challenge in store for me that broke my heart wide open.

There were no fences to protect me in the arena, and instead of just going to one horse, today we were letting the horses come to us. Our challenge was to stand by a randomly placed cone in the soft dirt while the facilitator let the herd in through the doors to amble to whomever they felt guided to. We were not to encourage them or move; we were just supposed to stand next to our cones. Feeling too vulnerable and shaky, I asked the training assistant Andrea if I could just watch. Andrea gave me a pep talk and convinced me that I would be safe and assured me that she would stand with me the whole time. I clutched her arm in a tight grip like I was about to fall off a forty-foot cliff. I stood by the cone as directed, my body shaking as I tried to breathe. I was incessantly talking with Andrea to calm down my breathing and the anxiety that was surging through me. My friend smirked as she watched me try to be brave and hollered from her cone, "You got this! They won't hurt you!"

The trainer opened the doors and the sunlight made me squint my eyes. I clutched on to Andrea and begged her not to leave me in some last-ditch effort to convey my nervousness about standing in the middle of an arena with five horses coming at me. I figured if I went to the farthest cone, I would have more time to warm up to the idea. Two of them came in and my trainer put her free hand over my trembling arm. As I shifted my attention to the horses, my cute blonde horse from yesterday's activities went to someone else. My logical mind kicked in to offer some comfort as I calculated that there were eight women and only five horses, maybe they would all just pass me by. That's when it happened.

The biggest horse in the herd was making a very deliberate beeline right for me. I jumped behind Andrea in an effort to disappear or at least delay the interaction. Surely the horse can't see me trembling behind the tall ranch hand. He walked around Andrea, so I had nowhere to hide. Gently he extended his nose to my trembling hand and I did my best to hold my hand out to him. I could feel his warm breath and the faint brush of his whiskers on my hand. Having him sniff my hand wasn't too intimidating, and I held it in place until he lifted his head and took a step forward.

"This is Thor. He wants you to touch his neck," Andrea explained as she reached her free hand to his neck. Seeing that Andrea's hand was still intact, I feebly reached out to Thor's beautiful auburn neck. His height was seventeen hands high and I barely came to his shoulder. I could feel the smooth soft hair under his black mane. I could feel the warmth of his skin and his soft pelt. He stood very still as I increased the breadth of my stroke down his neck. My heart slowed and I could feel his pulse. I started to shift from the rambling thoughts in my head and put my focus on my heart. He really was a beautiful horse. He lowered his neck and head slightly and made eye contact. I saw the gray dusting of lashes and his amber eyes looking at me.

"He likes you," Andrea encouraged me.

Looking into the eye I was closest to, I felt something in my body energetically shift. I could feel his gentle energy engulfing me and I suddenly realized why my daughter loved her horse so much. There was a very distinct connection that was almost inexplicable, or at least very difficult to convey with words. I took a deep breath as I continued to pet under his mane. In my mind I decided that this was manageable as long as Thor didn't move.

Of course, he did move and my heart rate increased immediately. I went right back into fear and grasped the air for Andrea's arm. I was too scared to watch where he was going. The horrific possibilities of what he was doing raced through my panic-stricken thoughts. He was making a circle around me and stopped for me to pet his neck again. This time, I forced myself to just take in the moment and breathe. I gently moved my hand from under his dark mane to his muscular shoulder. I had never actually petted a horse and I made myself step out of fear to take in the magnitude of this experience. Then he gently took one step forward. I felt like petting him was a big accomplishment and figured he was moving on to greet another one of the retreaters. I took a deep breath and apologized to Andrea for gripping her so tightly, thinking that I wasn't really as afraid after this interaction.

I heard him snort behind me and stiffened up again. He wasn't leaving as I had assumed. He was circling around me again but this time he aligned himself with my body so we were head-to-head when I turned around. With Andrea's patient guidance, I touched his soft velvet nose and felt the coarse hair around his nostrils. Then, everything changed. Thor had shifted his stance and moved lengthwise in front of me. Slowly, he started to bend his front knees. Not familiar with the nuances of horse behavior, I looked at Andrea, whose arm I had in my tight grip for some semblance of safety. As he crouched on his hind legs, Andrea called out to our facilitator, Sarina. I wanted to dart out of there, but Andrea put her arms around my shoulders when she felt my body shift. Thor snorted as he released his head and was laying at my feet. I looked up feebly at Andrea as my eyes filled with tears. I thought he was having some sort of health issue and I clearly had no idea what to do in this situation.

Sarina was suddenly beside me. "He wants you to lay with him," she said.

In my head I was gasping, *He wants what?* Having her repeat her words didn't seem to bring any clarity to what was happening or make my body want to cooperate. I wasn't really sure how to snuggle up to a horse and the logistics of where to put myself in relation to his exposed belly stirred up feelings of insecurity about how to handle this experience. I sat behind his front legs, and he lifted his head to look at me. I thought I was too close and considered getting back up, but Sarina encouraged me to continue, and he put his head back down on the ground. I extended my arms and gently leaned into him. My head fit at the base of his neck, and I made every effort to hug him. I could feel his soft fur on my cheek and feel his heart beating under my chest. He lifted his head and looked at me. He nuzzled his nose into my shoulder and exhaled. I heard Andrea's voice explain that he is hugging me back. My heart immediately softened, and I was completely overcome with emotion. He was still looking at me and my vision blurred as tears welled up in my eyes. I felt them drift down my cheeks into the soft nape of his neck, and I realized that I felt safe, and my mind had stopped racing. I was completely in this moment.

I'm not sure how long we laid there in the middle of the crowded arena looking at each other, but as my focus drifted from Thor's gaze to Sarina and Andrea standing nearby, I noticed they were both crying. I shifted my weight and pet his jaw and neck, overwhelmed with his patience and compassion, and realized that the other women had stopped what they were doing and were also watching this interaction transpire. The other horses started to approach us, and I felt Thor shift his weight to stand back up. I moved away so he could get his legs back under him. I was completely speechless. That was the most intense and beautiful experience I'd ever had! My fear of horses was completely eradicated at that moment. I couldn't put into words what had changed, but I knew this was an experience that marked a new perspective for me.

In our evening circle, Sarina explained that she had never seen any of her horses lay down before. It was very rare for a horse to do that, she said, especially since it makes them so defenseless – very risky behavior in a herd. For Thor, it was particularly monumental because he was a rescued horse that had been abused by his previous owner. For him to lay down in an arena with other horses present was a huge risk for him because he was completely vulnerable and defenseless, but he wanted me to know that he trusted me. My heart was flooded with gratitude in a way that I never knew was possible. I trusted him too and the intensity of that gesture by the tallest horse in the pasture to put himself at risk gave me some powerful insights about myself.

I learned that being vulnerable can be safe when done with love and support. If I didn't follow through with a completely open heart, I never would have known what I was capable of in terms of unconditional love. It was so empowering to soften my defenses and just be in each magical moment feeling Thor's heartbeat and having our breathing in sync instead of being in my head distressed with my fear. My heart completely broke open when he gave me a hug; it was the most powerful exchange of love and trust that I had really genuinely experienced in my life. I am not sure that I ever really was completely trusting another human being without being guarded in some capacity. Even as a mother, I found that I wanted to protect my kids or help them feel confident, so I kept some of my insecurities and fears to myself; especially when they were younger. This experience with Thor was when my lack of self-confidence completely shifted for me.

Thor taught me to look at situations without being so fearful of the unknown. Instead of letting others make decisions for me, it was okay to trust myself to be in the moment and trust my own choices. He was in an arena with other horses in the most vulnerable situation to show me that he trusted me and encouraged me to lay with him even though I was terrified; we were in our most vulnerable moment, together. He didn't have any guarantees that the other horses wouldn't come over, nor did he have any control over what I would do; he just allowed the situation to unfold and he did it with a completely open heart. I began to realize that there is no need for me to try to avoid new situations because of fear. It was time to redirect my life in a way that I kept my heart open and trusted not only myself, but to extend that to others around me.

I also learned that my fear of horses had nothing to do with the horse itself, it was more about my fear of trusting in my personal power. I had to start taking charge of my life and not relying on others to do a better job of taking care of me or my life than I can. I also had to stop the self-sabotage and step into my life with a little more confidence and less insecurity. I had never been that close to a horse, especially one so big! But somehow, I managed to figure out how to navigate how to lay on Thor in the middle of the arena. I had to be in the moment without being consumed with my doubts. It was a new realization that I was capable of trying new things and facing the fear of not being in control. I did have some guidance and support, but ultimately, I had to just go for it. I fumbled with the logistics, but because I tried, I had the most amazing experience of my lifetime.

I learned that it is okay for me to try new activities that scare me. I can still get help, but it was important for me to have clarity around the unhealthy way that I have been approaching new tasks by avoiding them altogether. It is okay if I am not an immediate expert at what I try. Just because someone else can do something well doesn't automatically mean that I am not capable of learning and integrating new skills. I just have to try while I am in my heart space and not in my critical headspace.

This is the string of my kite – the piece that connects all these pivotal parts of who I am and how I navigate the world. I can choose self-care and use my voice, but if I don't trust myself to stand in my personal power, I am not complete, even with the other tools I have. The pieces of the frame of the kite are important, but it won't fly without the string which is an ultimate trust in myself as a complete, and confident person living with an open heart. I realized that since I am with myself every minute of my life, I have to trust who I am. All of the tools in the world will not help me if I don't use them. When I feel uncomfortable or vulnerable, I realize that is when opportunity arises for me to stretch beyond the fears. I need to try new adventures without getting into fear about what I cannot control. This doesn't mean that I will put myself in dangerous situations, it means that I have shifted my fear so I can be open to what I am learning. Instead of having those feelings stop me, I step into the fear, trusting that this uncomfortable feeling will subside and a new awareness will emerge. Once I am in that state of being uncomfortable and I am successful, I feel empowered. Thor was my teacher for empowering myself to get the magic out of those uncomfortable moments in my life. I learned how to stay open and be in my heart rather than my head and it has made all the difference.

Chapter Eight

Trust in the Divine Timing

(Bow #1)

There was a time in my life when the thought of being alone made me spin with anxiety. If I was alone as a teenager, I had to have music playing, a book to read or the landline phone to connect with others. I would even clean my room to dull the emotions of fear and anxiety of being alone. Life has taught me otherwise. Being lonely and being alone are completely different emotions, each with its own energy vibration. I have been lonely before, especially after my divorce. Sitting alone with my errant thoughts and reflections used to make me spin into a tither of frustration. I have discovered that the alone time can be turned into quality time. We are sometimes conditioned to believe that we must constantly be with people or at activities. This is a culture that is always on the move and constantly bombarded with stimuli. We can get so distracted with phones and responsibilities and overrunning to-do lists that have us spinning like whirling dervishes.

What I have learned is that quality alone time can be very rejuvenating. It is imperative to take time out for your mental and physical health. If you don't, often your body will force you to with illness or injuries.

While socializing and interacting with others at work or at play are important, it needs to be in balance with solitude. Church was always a place to get the most of both worlds while I was growing up. I loved the community and the ritual of getting together each week to share time with members of the community. Catching up with friends during coffee hour was always enjoyable. Each week brought a different energy to the table. Some weeks were full of laughter, and some were a time to reach out for support or a hug.

It was nice to have a social place to be in reverence for the blessing of the week and enjoy each other's company. Church was also the place where I explored my relationship with God. While I was growing up, I was taught a sense of separateness between me and God. I was just the sinning child that had to keep track of and confess my wrongdoings every week. Over time my perspective changed. I felt as though my presence in church was for reverence and an awareness of my shortcomings that would potentially prevent me from salvation if not rectified and I was constantly second guessing everything that I did. I was perplexed by how I was taught to fear God, who is an abundant source of love. I was also inundated with uncertainties that made me very cautious about my choices and daily interactions. I always wondered if there was more than one way to live a faithful life, so I started exploring new perspectives.

My best friend in high school was of a different faith and going to her youth group gatherings gave me more of a feeling of being part of the bigger picture of God as a loving energy and I was curious how I could contribute my gifts to the world. This contrast made me reflect on my beliefs. It was different from what I had been taught in my church. There was more of a feeling of God as a guardian and constant support rather than a harsh judge of my life. It was a choice to welcome this interpretation into my life and rely on guidance which shifted my fears. I was even more awakened when I became part of a new church that my husband had grown up in.

I participated in classes with other new members to explore what the faith entailed. I became an active member in my husband's church which had an alternate view of our interaction with God. It was focused more on community service for others. With all these different experiences, I continued to explore my relationship with a higher power. I actually combined elements from all that I had learned in each congregation and formulated my own ideas about spirituality that feel more balanced to me. From my church as a child, I learned that I was on the planet to be mindful of my thoughts and actions and aware of consequences that affected my life after death. From my friend's church I learned not to fear God. I created more collaboration with the church teachings and how I interacted with people in my life that wasn't so fear-based and consumed with consequences for every thought and choice that I made. In my husband's church, I learned to be more community oriented and show my love of God through acts of service and kindness to others.

By merging what I felt was most useful for me from all of these church experiences, I stopped feeling separated from a higher power. The balance of faith became making a connection and realizing that I am a part of God and surrounded with higher vibrational beings that are always close and invested in my success here on earth. Whether you refer to the higher power as God, Spirit, Universal Power, or something else, it is always around you even if you are physically alone. I am surrounded by guardian angels that can help me, even if I don't know who they are. The key is that I need to be willing to ask for help. I learned this lesson at a very precarious moment in my life which confirmed my beliefs.

I was always thankful that my college roommate had a car. It seemed to add a little more freedom to our college shenanigans. Our cruiser was a sporty brown 1975 Plymouth Skamp. The two-tone stylish paint job continued on the inside where the creamy white seats were contrasted by the maroon-brown dashboard. It was a very large two-door with a small space in the back seat and a spacious bench seat in the front. The car was just a little quirky; I couldn't ever seem to open the passenger-side door. I would slam my shoulder into it to make a more aggressive attempt to open it, but I couldn't get it to budge, ever. Many attempts on several occasions failed to open the door no matter what method I chose, I could not penetrate the iron will of this door.

Opening from the outside was equally challenging, so I got in the habit of just hopping into the driver's side and sliding across the seat to be by the passenger door. Over time, the

Skamp became stubborn about not letting me open the door so we nicknamed it the Beast.

On this particularly sunny summer day, my roommate Rose and I were listening to music and enjoying our lively conversation. I was nuzzled into the corner of the door chatting with my her about what we should do next. The Beast was our vehicle of choice to go to the mall because of its spacious interior, we knew we could fit all of our new treasures inside, and we had quite a list of things we needed to furnish our new apartment.

As we turned the corner after the light had turned green, I was mid-sentence when the passenger door spontaneously flew open. I quickly grasped for the seat belt as my feet flew out from under me. I couldn't believe my head and chest were precariously dangling out of the Beast while we made a left turn. My hair was sweeping the small rocks on the pavement and after the initial shock had worn off and I realized what happened, I was completely flabbergasted that the door opened without any effort. My first inclination was to laugh that the Beast had just spit me out of the car, but then I had absolutely no strength anywhere in my core to lift me up. As I stared under the door, I could see the lines in the road and my initial feeling of surprise switched to a horrified state of terror. The inertia of the turn forced my body further out of the car and the seatbelt extended to put me closer to the pavement. I felt Rose's hand grasp my ankle, but it didn't give me the necessary leverage to pull myself back into the car. I was somewhere between hysteria and panic. Fear had ramped up and ominous scenarios of my body being horribly maimed on the road that was inches from my head, frantically rolled through my imagination. The seatbelt did not lock, so the more I pulled on it, the farther I was out the door; it was terrifying. As my bottom slid off the seat completely, I felt panic start to consume me. I didn't see this situation ending well, and I sent up a very desperate prayer for help.

At that moment, the door started to swing toward me; the inertia of the turn had created an aggressive momentum of the door to come toward my face which created a new set of problems. My head was hanging below the runner of the door, so having the door come at me meant that I risked the door hitting me in the face which would make me fall into the road. My other choice was to let go of the seatbelt which would also make me fall into the road and cause an accident. Neither scenario seemed beneficial to me, and I felt momentarily hopeless. The door was getting closer, and I needed to make my decision. Interestingly, the door stopped swinging even though we were still moving through our turn. The stubborn door was stuck in its position about a foot away from my face.

The door would not budge in either direction when I grabbed it; which was advantageous in this moment of panic. I reluctantly let go of my grip on the seatbelt and grabbed the inside of the window by the lock. I kicked my ankle free from my roommate's hands and put it back on the floor to get some leverage. I was able to put my weight on the door which was now stuck open. I moved my body into the car enough so that I was sitting on the edge of the door runner pressing my knee against the bottom of the dashboard and gripping the door window with one hand and the frozen door frame with the other hand. I was still not all the way in the car, but I felt safer without my head so close to the road. I could see the sheer panic on my roommate's pale face as she pulled into the first parking lot she could find. The car slowed down much faster than my heart rate did. My roommate immediately inquired about my well-being as she put the Beast into park. I assured her I was ok as I made my way back into the Beast and tried to pull -the door shut, but it was still stuck. I yanked it toward me with no success. I looked incredulously at my roommate and told her I couldn't get the door to close. Then we burst into that laughter – the kind that sounds like you're on the verge of hysteria and is great for releasing tension.

We laughed at the irony of how the door that never opened managed to break free at the worst possible time. Being in the center of a busy intersection was hardly an opportune time for the door to come ajar after all the times that I had practically dislocated my shoulder trying to force it open in the past which made us laugh even harder about the whole situation.

The fact that the door would not close was just more fodder for us to laugh about. I got out of the car and pushed the door with one hand and it closed immediately, with no resistance which made us ponder what it was even stuck open for. Then I realized that was the answer to my prayer. If I wasn't able to shift my weight using the door, I would not have made it back into the safety of the Beast. I determined after some consideration and review of this incident that one of my guardian angels held the door for me. So many variables contributed to each element of this incident, and many didn't add up with my analytical mind. I knew there were some higher powers at work that prevented this from turning into a bad accident. It was all the proof that I needed. I learned first-hand about the power of prayer and what it means for me in my daily life.

The beauty is that I don't have to just be in crisis when I ask for assistance, guidance, or help. In my human experience, it is easy to get into my ego and convince myself that I am the only one responsible for my experiences. What I have come to realize is that we all have guides, deceased loved ones and of course God that always wants to help. There are several instances in my life that I can recall where releasing fears or doubts and trusting in the Divine intervention changed the outcome of events. Of course, there is no way to prove it however, I truly believe that I am always supported. I just have to be willing to let go of what I perceive as control and ask for help and guidance and then stay open to receive. Dangling from the Skamp, I was wide open to receive any help to quell my terror.

I believe that we have free will in our human experience and that those in the angelic realm are always willing to help. This is why I believe in the power of prayer and why I put it as a bow on the kite. It's a little bonus to all of the other skills I am developing. It is my responsibility to open a dialogue by being in gratitude connecting with Source daily with prayer, journaling, ceremony, or meditation. It becomes a daily practice that keeps me connected and centered. I know that I have amazing people alive and deceased that are guiding me when I am open to receiving. I just have to be still and listen after asking for help. I have also found several resources of inspiration to help me daily, not just when I am in crisis. Practicing all of these tools at different times has been my way of connecting with my faith. I have made meditation part of my daily routine so I can connect and stay in gratitude. Once I block out the clutter, I can really focus on my intentions and what I am manifesting each day with journaling as well. I don't have to have the plan complete immediately after I pray or make a request to the universe, I can stay encouraged with mantras and positive self-talk. I just need to stay open to what I receive as I strive toward my goals.

I can plan until I am blue in the face and can still get blindsided with unanticipated fears which can make me feel defeated. It is great practice to put down the specifics and feelings around what I want to manifest, and then I have to let go of the details and trust that the situation will turn out for my highest good. I have learned to keep reflecting and working toward my goals and being mindful and grateful each step of the way. I know that I am supported and I trust the journey much more now rather than resisting it. More often than not, the universe can conjure scenarios and outcomes that can surpass my expectations if I stay aware and reflect.

Life experiences are more powerful for me if I react or think about what is actually happening and not worrying about what I think will happen. Most of the time, what I thought would transpire in situations throughout my life, didn't. I was so convinced that I had to figure everything out for myself because I was the only one steering the direction of my life. I now believe that I am a co-creator with spirit. I am not separate from the spirit realm. I am a spiritual being having a human experience. My belief in God has shifted, I don't believe He just threw me on the planet to muddle through my life. I was sent with loved ones to help me be of service and shine my light as often as possible. We all have separate journeys and things to accomplish here on Earth and we all come from the same Divine source of unconditional love. The soul in our bodies is the Divine energy pulsing through us as we navigate our life path. We can all tap into that Divine Source of unconditional love whenever we are scared or when we are connecting to our life purpose.

This is the first bow in the metaphor of the kite in my life. Letting go of the control and asking for help or guidance is what connects me to the Divine. Worrying about the future and trying to control how it will unfold is a waste of time. I used to think I had to control so many aspects of my life, when in reality the things I did not see coming were the most jarring and life changing like this door swinging open. When I least expected it, I was blindsided by events I couldn't fathom so it turned out to be a futile way to live. It was also in those moments that I was forced to get out of my head and trust in a higher power. There was no way for me to assume that door would open, ever. But in the instant, when there was so much chaos, unexplainable events transpired that helped me back into the car. With my faith in the Divine, I am empowered to achieve my life purpose with the power of prayer and belief that I am being guided and supported with unconditional love.

Chapter Nine

Be Honest with Yourself, You Always Have a Choice!

(Bow #2)

*I*n my youth the statement that I could do anything I wanted to with my life gave me a feeling of ultimate freedom. My preadolescent ideas of what my life looked like were only limited by my imagination. Twirling in my ballet dress conjured up fantasies of flapping my wings in Swan Lake. I never had to worry about the details of how I was going to accomplish such a fantasy, I just pictured myself there and enjoyed the feelings I imagined would surge through me on the stage in front of a sold-out crowd at David H. Koch theater in New York City. Everywhere I looked I was inspired. My ideas shifted daily based on what movie I watched or what activity I participated in. As I got older, my aspirations became more detailed and complex but still lacked any cohesive plan on how to actually sustain any of these fantasies. They became more tempered when adults stopped praising my creativity and began to share some disdain for my choices based on their fears of not making enough money or not being realistic enough. That's when I got out of my heart of creativity and leaped into a head full of doubts and fears that didn't originate with me, even if I internalized them.

I had played out scenarios of my choices with such detail, I gave myself analysis paralysis. Many times, it was difficult for me to even make a decision because I was concentrating on extraneous details that were not even in existence yet, aimlessly trying to cut them off before they actually happened to protect myself. This often gave me anxiety because I did not know how to control all of the variables or how to anticipate all of the possibilities. However, as I started to shift my perspectives, I learned that if I am always comfortable and safe, I am not learning or growing. I also tend to cut off new experiences because of fear which shuts down my capacity to love and live authentically. It is a powerful mindset to look at change as an opportunity.

Change used to trigger me into fear and resistance. What I learned is that fear and resistance never stopped changes from occurring, so I had to rethink how I felt about change since it is inevitable. I learned that change is about letting go of what no longer serves me or helps me expand so I learned how to embrace it. The art of letting go is not always easy, but it is necessary. There comes a time in your life when you need to be honest with yourself and totally unapologetic for who you are. I had spent so much time trying to be the perfect wife, and perfect mother and perfect career woman that I lost sight of my own journey. I didn't realize how far off of my path I had veered until I was out in public for the first time since news of my divorce had become common knowledge when I had an a-ha moment.

I was at my son's baseball game and the tension in the bleachers was palpable. I normally sat on the sidelines in my fold-out chair sipping an iced tea, but on this cool April day I glanced over and saw my soon-to-be-ex sitting there. I needed to find a different place to watch the game. It was as if I was transported back to those middle school days at a new school, wondering where I should sit in the lunchroom. My stomach knotted up and I felt awkward; part of me even wished I wasn't there. It was just one of those intensely uncomfortable moments I found myself in after the town caught wind of our divorce.

I made my way under the cover of the bleachers. Each step I took on the metallic stairs seemed to reverberate and announce my presence. I felt all eyes on me as I visually navigated where I would be able to sit. I sensed that there were many that had some ideas about our situation, and I really didn't feel like I had the energy to explain or defend myself about why the divorce was happening.

I started up the stairs, unable to soothe my trepidations as I scanned the crowd for a place to sit and enjoy the game. Everyone had a place nestled in with their families or friends, and I felt like I was encroaching on owned land. This was definitely a test of my resilience. I didn't want to shove myself in the thick of the crowd and have to chitchat. I had to refocus and remember that I was here to support my son and make it look as seamless for me as possible so he wouldn't be distracted.

I could still feel the eyes of the others tracking me as I made my way to the sparsely-populated top section. I was only two rows behind the majority of the crowd so I wasn't isolated, and I felt like I could at least focus on the game without the stress of being within the energy of the other fans. As I nestled in my spot, I could feel the knot in my stomach writhing in my gut.

I tried to engage in the game, but my head was a jumbled mess. Part of me was wondering if I made the right decision to come sit in the bleachers. The other part was a little annoyed that I wasn't able to just go to my spot along the third base line in my chair, but I knew that this was part of my decision to get a divorce and I needed to put on a brave face and concentrate on the game. I wasn't as exuberant with my cheering from this vantage point, but I was enjoying seeing my son have some fun with his friends. I saw him scan the bleachers while he warmed up to bat and I made sure to wave and smile. Hopefully it brought him some comfort knowing that I was at the game. Although I secretly hoped he could not tell how tortured I felt sitting there.

I didn't want to draw any more attention to myself than was already attaching to me. I heard the chatter and cheers among the fans, and again was keenly aware that this was my first outing since the town got the memo about our divorce. Though inevitable, it was uncomfortable to actually be there grappling with all of my errant thoughts and feelings in this setting. I always felt like a bit of an outsider, not having grown up in this town. I did my best to fit in but there were a lot of unspoken rules that I seemed to bump into and today I was acutely aware that my position in the community had changed. I had plans to move closer to the city where I taught, and I felt a pang of sadness that I wasn't going to have many of these people in my daily life anymore. I was currently juggling where I was and where I was going in my life. I was definitely at a crossroads, and the stress was building up in my body. I would miss a lot of what I had come to know over the past twenty years, and it was hard for me to be in the moment. I was glad that I had the game to focus on. I was also comforted by the fact that I could see everyone in front of me and didn't have to worry about who was behind me.

My attention was diverted when I noticed Ganine, the mother of one of my son's close friends, coming up toward me. The metal clang of the bleachers under her feet made it easy to track as she sat down beside me. I thought it was nice of her to come say hello. We intermittently chatted and cheered on the batters as they went up to the plate, but I felt my stomach getting tighter. I didn't think my body could assimilate much more anxiety and I was thinking of excusing myself to go to get some snacks when she asked the dreaded question.

"Why are you two getting divorced? What happened?"

The crowd seemed to take a collective inhale as I paused to ponder how to answer her. My head started swimming for what was appropriate to say. I had many scenarios and ideas that I could relay that would help others see the situation from my point of view, but my husband grew up in this town and it didn't seem necessary to hurt him or damage his reputation.

Also, I was just as responsible as he was. What a difficult question to answer diplomatically here behind home plate. I could tell that others were curious as a hush came over the crowd, which made me even more uncomfortable. I'm sure only a few seconds transpired while I frantically rushed through my thoughts to placate the curious people that were at the game, but it felt like my silence had eaten up at least ten minutes.

I had come here from a big city and living in the country, with a twenty-minute commute to work and back each day. The drive had given me a lot of time to think and arrive at this decision. My time in the car was used to decompress from the rigors of the workday or to fire up for the household duties awaiting me at home. I felt the shifting from how I was going to use my time without so many extraneous factors to consider every time that I wanted to do something. I knew I needed to get back in balance with myself and what I wanted to do with my life.

Of course, there were so many layers to why we are getting divorced and hashing out what I felt or did or didn't do in front of a crowd here in the bleachers at my son's game seemed like a bad idea. I had a lot of emotion that was trying to bubble to the surface and the effort I put in to even coming here seemed to deplete what little energy I had. I struggled to keep my feelings in check. I knew I was going to have to release so many aspects of what I had grown to enjoy in my life and I was emotionally torn in so many areas. I knew that if I opened the gates, I would completely lose it.

I realized that I didn't need to defend myself and it wasn't necessary for the people in the stands to have any input or comment about what was transpiring in our lives. My seat at the top of the bleachers was not a sacred space to share my heart and I didn't want anything I said to be fodder for the next few months. But I didn't want to be rude and as the blood rushed to my face and neck, I prayed for something to come to me. Suddenly, I heard myself say, "I just decided to stop pretending to be something I am not."

I feel like I had tried to give my children a good balance of city and country life but now that they were both grown up, I felt like I had to step into some new version of myself that wasn't sitting in this small town pretending to be a dutiful farm wife for the rest of my life. I was sick of commuting and having two separate lives with work there and my family here. I had never really pin-pointed the reason why I needed to move on until I heard myself say it out loud in the bleachers. All of the other incidents and reasons that I arrived at this boiled down to the core of who I had become. I had shaved down so much of my personality and hid my intuitive abilities for fear of being ostracized or having my children be teased. I just could not be that person anymore. I had to be true to myself and it wasn't necessary to berate my ex-husband or any of the friends I had made over the years. I was the problem, and this was the solution. I knew I was making the right choice even though it was difficult.

There wasn't much to work with in terms of keeping the conversation going and Ganine had a blank look on her face like I had just slapped her with a fish. Some of the parents looked back at me and I sheepishly smiled. And in a moment of mercy, my son looked up to the stands to ask if he could get some snacks. I didn't even realize the game had ended. Thankful for an exit, I excused myself and hopped down the bleachers to join him. That was so uncomfortable on so many levels, but what I realized is that as painful as this transition was going to be, it was important to stop pretending. I had to just own who I am. I had to trust that we all would be okay and grow from the changes that were inevitably transpiring. I needed to let go and trust God.

It is such a simple sentiment in concept but living through it and staying in trust was a challenge. I had to start flying in a new breeze. Time has been an elixir for the seismic shift I seemed to initiate and the months following the changes were difficult to navigate. The fact is that I have met some really kind and generous people in that town and have enjoyed the small community where I knew my kids were safe and I could call many people if I needed anything at all. I was finally in a place where I could create a home and stop constantly moving as I had done growing up. But after twenty years, the idea that I would never move ironically started to haunt me. I was not really feeling like this was where I wanted to spend my time without the kids and their activities. The energy of the town didn't seem to be where I was vibrating anymore and I had to figure out what to do with whatever is left of my life. It wasn't the town or the people, it was me. I needed something else and I just couldn't worry about what everyone else was saying or thinking. I had to take time to get to know myself all over again. To explore new interests and get into a new vibration that matched where I wanted to be. I didn't need approval or understanding. I just leaned into trusting my own thoughts and feelings and honoring them.

There is a bow on the kite because honoring who you are on all levels is an important tool for living authentically. We are on this planet to contribute with our gifts and learn from our challenges. I had to honor who I am and not worry about how it looks to other people. The people I am meant to be with will appear. I am no longer interested in hiding who I am or trying to fit into a mold of what others expected me to be.

The bows of your kite are the tools you use to help you recalibrate when you are moving through more emotional experiences. To really create joy in your life, it is important to feed your interests and add more bows to decorate your kite string. I love taking classes and meeting like-minded people that are supportive and energetic. I think any class you are drawn to increases your self-awareness which is a powerful tool for living authentically. Some of my favorite memories are at healing retreats. They can be intense because I am usually letting go of what no longer serves me; and meeting some resistance because that was one of my strongest strategies before I knew there were others. Holding on to what I know and jumping into an abyss and just trusting the experience was not a comfortable way for me to navigate through my life. I created a belief that it wasn't safe to have my weaknesses exposed or talk about my pain or sadness and I had the exact opposite experience. I have met some of the most loving generous men and women in that vulnerable state and it changed how I live my life.

When you look at the possibilities and find powerful mentors you will increase the feelings of empowerment and be able to take charge of your life. Stay curious and keep exploring new interests to gain more tools! There are amazing mentors and teachers that will inspire you with their journey and growth. You can also become a "heartist" in any way that feeds your interests. A heartist is someone who participates in creative and active pursuits they love. This will help you stay balanced with work and play and constant growth and expansion. You can get into a group that loves hiking or biking, planting herbs or even expressing your creativity in problem solving at work. Your exploration is only limited to your imagination. All activities that encourage you to explore your interests and meet other like-minded people that like to do that will be so important for you and will add new bows to your kite.

Chapter Ten

The Key to Happiness is Self-Love! (The key)

ove is the key to happiness because that is the elixir for your shadows, fears, and insecurities. It can also heal you physically and emotionally. Over my lifetime, I have heard this sentiment spoken in several ways. I thought of myself as loveable, but I was really stretched out of my comfort zone at a retreat where we delved into what self-love really consists of. We had to do some mirror work, which turned out to be far more powerful than I anticipated. I'd spent a lot of time in front of that reflective surface during my life, but it was never quite like this.

We were all given a mirrored tile and told to look into it and tell your reflection you love her. Not a difficult proposition in theory. Of course, I thought I loved myself, but I wasn't really in love with the reflection. My pupils shifted in size as I tried to focus on the face staring back at me. I immediately started to see the flaws in my skin. The wrinkles starting to flank my eyes and how faded my make-up had become and I realized that this was a pattern for me. I had never really been kind to myself in a mirror. My first instinct when I held the mirror to my reflection was to get into critical mode and zero in on what I considered my shortcomings and flaws. I put my face very close to my magnified mirror so I could see more than the naked eye ever could. In an effort to follow through with this challenge, I tried to focus on my eyes and stop distracting myself by falling into old patterns of self-criticism. I saw the shift in my pupils as I let the extraneous details of my face fade. I looked deeply into my eyes, and then I just focused on one.

There was an air of intensity, and I could see my eyes in close detail. I don't think I have ever looked into my own eyes with compassion. I could see the dark blue ring encircling the gold and brown flecks in the green and yellow iris. This assignment was to eradicate all of those negative feelings about how I look and I found it very challenging. As I looked into my eyes and started to say I love you my eyes immediately began to sting with tears. I couldn't believe it was this hard. If I expected other people to love me, why couldn't I do it for myself? I have always been able to see the shortcomings and flaws and managed to emotionally beat myself up for looking or feeling differently than I do. I tried to hold my emotions back and became self-conscious that I was having such a hard time. I have been told I was loved, but I never realized how important it is to truly love myself. I could not seem to stifle the tears that were emerging from my eyes and rolling down my cheeks. I was so exasperated and confused by the visceral reaction I had to saying I love you to my reflection. What an interesting paradox for me that I could easily say it to others but could not seem to express the sentiment to my reflection. This was such an insight to how mean I am to myself, every day.

Picking out all of my self-inflicted flaws, the mirror had never been a place for me to be vulnerable and open to receiving love. I was able to realize in this moment that it had been a place for me to be critical and cruel to my changing body. I reinforced the dysmorphic image of myself that I was too fat or needed to blend in my freckles or I have a pointy chin and the constant comparison I was in with my other family members or famous people in society that I failed to recognize my own beauty. It had never occurred to me to go to the mirror and tell myself anything positive until this day. I couldn't seem to say I love you out loud, but when I said it in my head while looking in the mirror, I noticed that my pupils pulsed and changed size. My body was actually reacting to the thoughts and words I was expressing, and I realized how detrimental this practice of self-loathing was to myself physically and emotionally. I walked out of that retreat vowing to be kinder to myself and keep doing the mirror work. It was a new daily practice of getting into my heart space and stop my critical thoughts. I taped a motivating mantra on the mirror in my bathroom and tried to recite it whenever I was spending time in front of it.

It took a few weeks for me to squeak out I love you without sparking tears. As it became easier, I started to add to my mantra; "I love you and the way that you are a light in the world. I love the body that God has chosen for me to be my vessel in this lifetime" After time elapsed with this daily practice, I challenged myself to go farther. It wasn't just my face in the mirror that I had to love. I started to look at my whole body. The scars and changes that have accumulated gave me pause. I had to stop seeing only the negative and began to realize what amazing experiences my body has endured in this lifetime. This was the first unique connection I had to each of my children. I had to see that for the miracle that it was and not focus on the stretch marks left behind. The scars and subtle changes all tell the story of my life. It was an intentional practice to reframe how I felt about my body and start to be thankful and truly love myself especially if I expected others to be able to love me. It took some diligence, but I started to feel a change in how I regarded myself. Once I had the awareness of how hard I was on myself, I knew I had work consistently to shift it.

It is not about being cocky or above anyone else, it is recognizing the light within you as easily as you can see the light in others. As I have heard several times, I am a spirit having a human experience. I believe that we are all pieces of the Divine put into a human body to be a part of this existence. Once I was able to love myself, I noticed several changes in my daily interactions with others. I am not so quick to be critical or judgmental of other people or where they are on their journeys. I am also able to have more compassion and patience with people and don't have as many triggers because loving myself has healed a lot of my tendencies to focus on the outside world. I started from within and worked my way outward and that strategy has helped me rely more on myself to build my self-esteem.

Self-love was about creating a healthy mindset that is the most integral part of my life. I was no longer dependent on outside validation, and it forced me to stop being so worried about what others think about what I look like. I realized that self-love is about really honoring the spirit inside me that is from God. My soul is uniquely encapsulated in the body that I have, and my criticism was negating the love that I have within me to express with the people around me. I started to realize that we are all inherently lovable because we are created from the highest source of love to be a light in this world. We are all from love. We return to that unconditional love when we leave our bodies and recognizing that for yourself while you are alive is a great source of healing. If you haven't tried mirror work, I encourage you to do it. Loving myself and honoring my body have been enormous shifts for me. I found myself wanting to be in nature more and being more active with my body. I actually spent time in my body being present and grounded and honoring it as a unique container for a most loving source of energy. I started to crave exercise and activity to keep myself strong and healthy. I cleaned up my diet and am mindful of what will nourish my body, not just squelch hunger. These shifts in my mindset have made all the difference in how I approach my day and honor my body, instead of criticizing it.

This is the key on your kite because it is another powerful tool of reversing some of the self-loathing and criticism that we seem to be socialized into believing as we grow up. It was easy for me to get distracted with the need for extraneous acceptance, but I never really felt that was a constant that I could count on. What I have learned is that it is not necessary for anyone else to validate my worth. It was up to me to mute the negative self-talk. I enveloped all parts of who I am and moved forward with my day knowing that I am lovable and learned how to fill my own cup so I am not completely drained each day. I am much more kind to myself now and have been able to shift the mindset of never being enough to recognizing my potential to love myself and others more freely.

Chapter Eleven

Take Flight!

Thank you for sharing the journey of how I created a more authentic and joy-filled life. I use the metaphor of a kite because, much like life, the building and flying of kites involve many facets and layers of learning. Each situation is an opportunity to reflect and incorporate new ideas or release old stories and patterns that make it hard to move forward. With both kites and with life, this takes intention and patience. It is easy to get mired down by bad weather and other events, but all it takes is a shift in mindset to soar above any storm.

When creating your life, you must, first and foremost, make yourself a priority. You get to choose where you want to put your time and energy, so do it with intention. I was a colander of energy for most of my life until I figured out that I needed to make my emotional needs a focus for my well-being. I know it can't be all about you all of the time – we all have loved ones and other responsibilities to consider. This is just a reminder to keep your needs within the framework of your daily routine. Love yourself enough to remember that you are valuable and take the time to recharge.

When I am in a situation that triggers me emotionally, I take time to look within and figure out what is being activated. A visceral reaction to a situation can be a sign that I need to heal, so I make sure I am listening and tuning into my feelings. Take the time to reflect and do what you can to learn from any situation that stirs up those uncomfortable moments. Remember that life is happening for you, not to you, and when you are challenged, try to observe the situation as objectively as you can so you don't inadvertently soak up all of the negative emotion.

I was brought up internalizing many beliefs that made me reluctant to communicate what I was feeling. Once I learned to honor my feelings and express them, I opened up to new experiences that made me aware of the need for an even exchange of energy with friends and loved ones. I have learned that I can give freely and love those around me without draining every ounce of energy that I have. I now make that a priority, knowing that what I am putting out into the world is being reflected back at me. I am not arrogant about it, just mindful that my energy is a gift that I get to share. It is also a gift that I can receive from others. Longevity is not guaranteed, and each interaction and choice I make has a profound effect on my life and those around me.

Find your voice and use it in a loving way to set boundaries and express your feelings. When you have feelings, honor them. Boundaries do not have to be concrete bulky divisions that you create to keep people away from your heart space. They are parameters that you create to control the influx of energy coming at you daily. Tune into your own inner guidance to help you navigate the situations that arise. Ask for clarity and use any tools that you can to heighten your intuition. We all have intuition. It can show up so many ways such as a feeling in your stomach or the hair on your neck standing up as a reaction to a conversation or situation. Somehow as children we are conditioned to relinquish our reliance on it, convincing ourselves that we just have to trudge through our lives and make decisions in our heads. Isn't it a comfort to know that you are supported and guided? You have a whole team of loved ones that are cued up and ready to help, you just have to ask and then listen. You can ask for signs that can help validate what you are experiencing. Signs from the Divine come in a variety of ways. Some insights come as an inner knowing, or you can see signs such as a cardinal or hear chimes ringing that you connect with a loved one. I asked my guides for big, obvious signs, because I know myself well enough to realize that I will miss a feather or a penny in the street. I also have a tendency to second guess if it is actually a sign or just my imagination, so I have asked my team to bump up their game a little. For example, while contemplating a new job opportunity I asked to see an orange balloon to confirm if it was the right decision. I figured that was random enough, and as I was driving down the interstate the next day, a hot air balloon with three shades of orange rose above the horizon! I had the answer I needed, and there was no second-guessing because it was so specific and exactly what I had asked to see.

Keep your channel open by being in gratitude and meditate or pray daily to keep yourself connected and in the higher energy vibrations. Play with your intuition and discover how you can communicate. I love setting an intention to hear a message on the radio before I get into my car. I remember when I moved from North Dakota to Colorado I was not sure if I was taking the right step forward in my life. The move was a huge undertaking, and I was exhausted from packing. The kids came into town to help me on the long drive cross-country in a large moving van. We spent the night on air mattresses in the living room after everything was stuffed into the moving van. I was filled with mixed emotions and second-guessed my decision the whole night. There was comfort in being a part of this community, and the friends I had made were hard to say goodbye to. I also loved my house and wished that I could move it with me. This was contrasted with my excitement to be closer to my kids, which was my main motivation for moving.

After hours of tossing and turning I realized that it was time to release this home and neighborhood so I could welcome in new adventures and get away from the sad memories that seemed to swirl in the woodwork of this home. Now staring at the empty walls and feeling the emotional void within the house, I realized that there was no reason to torture myself over my decision anymore. I just had to trust that the details of this move were all going to come together.

Yes, part of me wanted to sit in anxiety and panic, but I knew that God and my guides and loved ones would not open all the doors to get me to this point only to leave me hanging.

I had to keep telling myself to trust that the Universe was conspiring to help me make a smooth transition. When the sun rose, I reluctantly crawled off the air mattress to make the final preparations. As I sat in the seat of the moving van, I asked for a hassle-free drive and a sign to remind me that what I was doing was for my highest good. Just then, I turned on the radio and the Boston song "Don't Look Back" was playing! I knew that was the confirmation I needed. It was time to look forward, and I cranked up the stereo as I pulled out of my driveway for the last time.

What I have come to realize is that I cannot work the tools if I do not practice them every day. When I do not, I have to take another look at my mindset, and usually find I have fallen back into old patterns and fears that are stifling my desires and draining my energy. What I now recognize is that there is a awareness to discern between lying to myself to silence the noise and empowering myself to focus my energy on so my highest good will transpire. Shifting your mindset is the strongest tool you can possess to feel empowered in your life. You can design it any way you want; it all comes down to choice. How you feel is a choice. How you react and move forward is a choice. How you treat yourself when faced with challenges is a choice. You are empowered to dictate how the experiences you have are going to be interpreted. When you use your tools to have a positive impact on how you digest those experiences, you are not just getting through each day, you become an active participant in your life.

Remember that joy is also a choice. You have to create it and relish it when you're feeling it. I create mantras to reinforce what I am thankful for and focused on creating, and that helps me raise my energy when I start to sink into my fears and depression. When I feel stuck, I ask myself, "What is one action that I can take today to shift the energy and help me move forward?" Just one step was all I could focus on during some of my darker days, but it was enough to start building momentum. For each step you take, your loved ones and guidance will take ten steps toward you to help you live your best life. Trust the guidance and keep moving forward, even if it is in stormy weather. Honor your body during the darker times too. Sometimes you just need to rest or be in silence so you can recalibrate from grief or heartache. Ignoring those feelings will not benefit you in the long run. You want to encourage them to come to you and go through you so you can move toward your next step when you choose to.

Allow the path to unfold and twist and turn without getting caught up in the details and negativity. The journey is where the golden nuggets are. I have learned that when I am clear on why I am doing something and I am not too attached to the specific outcome, it is easier for me to trust that what is transpiring is happening for me and my life is unfolding in magical ways. No, it's not all unicorns and sparkles, as we humans we can experience truly painful and difficult situations. I have learned to take it one step at a time and to keep breathing. I do not take as long to recalibrate when the unexpected happens because I can reframe incidents that are not as pleasant and see what I am healing and learning about myself.

Take the time and effort to construct your life as you would your kite: in a way that enables flight. If you have followed the metaphor set out in this book, you can see how making yourself a priority builds your foundation. It's how you put your support in place by choosing your boundaries and owning your personal responsibility in situations. You can use your voice to make positive change in your life and to make your desires and feelings known as well. There is no reason to be disingenuous to yourself and struggle to do everything alone or suffer in silence; let love in and live with an open heart. In addition, putting yourself first means that you are choosing yourself to be your priory in thought, emotion, and activity. You are empowered when you recognize that everyone is responsible for their own feelings, and it is not up to you to change or fix anyone because we all have choices. You "do you" and don't absorb what is not yours. You can be compassionate, but you don't have to be a sponge.

Creating a sisterhood of support and encouragement is so important to raise your vibration and heal. It is also a great awareness that you are powerful and can access the gifts you have where it is safe to explore. This is the fabric of your kite. You cannot let the dream-stealers and negative people pull your kite down. Let them go and trim your kite so it will fly freely. It needs to be trimmed and fitted to allow your kite to fly; it is your own personal journey. Don't be afraid to step away from people or activities that no longer serve you. You can rely on the fact that others will come into your life who support and share your interests. Do your best to stay away from people who do not align with your dreams so you don't shelve them.

Don't try to hold on to toxic people or their judgments and criticism either. Realize that it is okay if other people let you go too. It may hurt at first, but when you believe that the Universe is conspiring to help you then you know you are creating space for new experiences. Trust yourself and your choices and listen to your intuition, friends, family, and your body—always. Create your boundaries and honor them by being honest with yourself and how much you want to juggle each day. No can be a complete sentence and can empower you to direct where you want your energy to go. Resist the urge to defend yourself, or make excuses for what you want or feel. Be honest with yourself too; fix what you can and do your best to stop getting your validation of worth and self-esteem from outside sources.

Learn from your life and recognize what is happening for you on a daily basis. Every experience helps us grow, and when you let that love flow to you and from you, you will find your path. Follow it with renewed vigor and excitement. Take steps toward a new goal or vision, but don't get too derailed if it takes more time or if you have to redefine it along the way, there is always Divine timing which supersedes our earthly time constraints. When your kite gets tangled with grief or other powerful emotions, reflect on them and feel them; do not stuff them or discount them. All emotion is energy, each with its own vibration which cannot be destroyed, only shifted. Your emotions are also messengers for your soul to help you clear and raise your vibration. Once you have the awareness, sort what you are learning and try a new tactic; ask for help if you need it. Don't be so quick to discount the need for others in your life, after all, we are not on the planet alone.

Exploring your interests and reflecting on your daily interactions will be the game-changer for empowering yourself to live an amazing and authentic life. Keep your energy on what you want to feel as you are manifesting, and focus on what is going well as often as you can. Do your best to stay in gratitude and give yourself grace when you are moving through tough life situations. The vibration you emit being your authentic self is magnetic – you will attract what you desire or something better that you didn't even know was possible. If challenges arise or feelings get overpowering, recalibrate using your tools to gain perspective and heal. Remember, life is cyclical and each challenge is for you to gain awareness and elevate your energy. Each life experience also has layers, so don't get discouraged if the same issue bubbles up again with different players. You will notice that as you heal those layers, you don't take as long to get your footing again and that is how you know your vibration is rising.

When you step into your day or a new challenge, picture yourself in an open field, full of possibilities, and all the wonderful experiences and hopes you have planted. Listen to the birds around you. Smell the fragrant flowers. Feel the gentle breeze on your face and the earth energy pulsing through your feet. Stay connected to Source and grounded to the earth's energy simultaneously so you can be a conduit of all of that love and light. When the sun is warm on your skin and that air is just right, let your kite string unwind and release your kite into the beautiful blue sky and manifest your dreams. No need to run or rush around, just slowly let out the string and watch your kite find the perfect current of air. Enjoy the sight of your kite dancing and swirling in the sky. Resist the urge to tug or force the direction in any way. Let the air be the angels and your loved ones who uplift you and support your dreams and the life you are manifesting. Now, let go, and let your life take flight!

Acknowledgments

Throughout my journey I have been blessed to have amazing friends, mentors, and supporters who inspired my transformation. I have shifted my way of processing life events by infusing the inspiration and teachings of some very powerful teachers and loving friends who support me so I stay balanced in mind, body, and spirit. By infusing these new perspectives and skills, I have become more empowered to live authentically.

To my mentor and soul sister, Sunny Dawn Johnston, who is a living example of unconditional love and encouragement. Sunny walks her talk and is truly authentic with all people, in all situations. Through many retreats, classes, travels and mentoring sessions, Sunny has taught me many strategies for reframing situations with my mindset and finding the lessons so I can uncover my light. She is so generous about meeting me where I am and guiding me past my comfort zone to an amazing awakening. I know she genuinely cares about me and tirelessly holds space for me to be the best version of myself. I am eternally grateful for her inspiration, teachings, and friendship. She is the person I go to for guidance, especially when I need a spiritual kick in the buns. She has seen me through really low times and always offered a warm loving hug, virtually and in person. I have trusted her with my fears and insecurities and she has met me with integrity and unconditional love every step of my way and reminds me that when I am nervous, to focus on service.

To my mentor and friend, Melissa Kim Corter, who was kind enough to write the foreword for this book. She is a woman of integrity and transparency who creates potent learning experiences from her wealth of knowledge. She has taught me how to feel safe in my body and how to set healthy boundaries to empower myself. Her dedication to sharing her knowledge and demonstration of leadership has been integral to many of the breakthroughs that I have experienced. Her connection with nature and the Divine Feminine have also been pivotal in my personal growth and expansion. I knew from that first day, when we sat at a small table at the back of a conference hall chatting and finding commonalities in our experiences, that she was a gift to my life. I am so thankful for our friendship, Melissa. You have been an incredible source of inspiration, helping me expand my awareness beyond what I ever knew existed. You supported my desire to embrace all facets of my shadows and my light and have been patient and conscientious about where I am on my journey.

To my sister and bad-ass friend, Stevie Famulari Gds. You are the person I can reach out to any time of day to be reminded how far I have come, to cry, to laugh or to manifest with GEL. I love that we call each other in crisis and in celebration with the same enthusiasm. We have had so many discussions in all stages of our journeys, comforting one another and also pointing out when we are recreating old stories. Thank you also for sharing your talents as a visionary artist to create the kite illustrations in this book. I am so grateful you have joined me and supported me on my path and have let me do that for you too.

To my publisher and friend, Shanda Trofe, who tirelessly and expertly assisted me in bringing this book to fruition. Her company, Transcendent Publishing, has been so professional and patient as I traversed the path to becoming a published author. I had so much healing to do and she reminded me to trust the Divine Timing of this book. During this amazing, decade-long personal journey, she let me experience the creative process and gave me time to integrate the lessons that I express within the book with endless patience and encouragement. Shanda was consistently grounded and offered me a sense of security, and her wealth of publishing knowledge helped this process feel seamless.

To Alaskan singer/songwriter Libby Roderick, a huge thank you for your generosity in letting me quote your song "How Could Anyone?" in this book. Your words are a life-lasting inspiration for authentic living. I had some of my most powerful and heartening reflections listening to your songs. You have a beautiful way of expressing some of the most complex emotions with simplicity, leaving room for your listener to expand self-awareness and connect to universal love.

About the Author

Lisa Eleni is a spiritual heartist, international best-selling author, intuitive tree reader, and Mind-Body-Spirit practitioner. She is the founder of Heartistry and Herbs, which focuses on empowering women by creating a safe space of love, support, and healing through meditation, art, journaling, herbs, oils and sprays and several self-awareness techniques. Lisa also hosts intentional woman's heartshops where we create a specific craft for the month. We set our intentions based on the monthly theme, and our creations hold the energy and remind us to keep moving toward our goals. Lisa also has various retreats for like-minded people to befriend and support each other. Her passion is encouraging women who desire a more joy-filled life and who want to live authentically. Lisa resides in Colorado.

For more inspiration and the latest information on artshops and new publications, contact: lisa@lisaeleni.com

Take Action!

Mantras are a great tool for encouraging you along your journey and helping shift energy to keep your vibration high. Download your free pdf of powerful mantras to empower you and keep you motivated to continue to grow and expand!

lisaeleni.com/freegift